CONSUMERISM AND THE MOVEMENT OF HOUSEWIVES INTO WAGE WORK

For my parents.

Consumerism and the Movement of Housewives into Wage Work

The interaction of patriarchy, class and capitalism in twentieth century America

DAVID R. WELLS

Ashgate

Aldershot • Brookfield USA • Singapore • Sydney

Published by
Ashgate Publishing Ltd
Gower House
Croft Road
Aldershot
Hants GU11 3HR
England

Ashgate Publishing Company
Old Post Road
Brookfield
Vermont 05036
USA

British Library Cataloguing in Publication Data
Wells, David R.
    Consumerism and the movement of housewives into wage work :
    the interaction of patriarchy, class and capitalism in
    twentieth century America
    1. Women consumers - United States 2. Women consumers -
    Research - United States 3. Women - Employment - United
    States 4. Women - Employment - Research - United States
    5. Social classes - United States
    I.Title
    331.4'21'0973'0904

Library of Congress Catalog Card Number: 98-73505

ISBN 1 85972 446 9

Printed and bound by Athenaeum Press, Ltd.,
Gateshead, Tyne & Wear.

Contents

Figures and tables

Acknowledgements

I want to first thank my wife, Rochelle, for her support emotionally and in helping proofread and edit this manuscript. Of course, after reading chapter five, one consequence will be that we will have many conversations on improving the household division of labor in our own marriage.

I also want to thank those who critiqued an earlier manuscript, which was my doctoral dissertation. The comments of Nora Hamilton, John Elliott, and Michael Messner were most appreciated. Nora, as my dissertation advisor, eagerly and promptly read many drafts of the work in progress and always provided useful advice, especially with respect to organization.

Two helpers, who took turns nestling comfortably at my feet, our dogs, Ruby and Jeremiah, certainly made the hours of 'solitary' writing more enjoyable. Whenever I turned the computer on, they would both come running to see who would get under the desk first and who would take residence on a bare spot of carpet. However, in the time between the completion of the dissertation and this manuscript, Jeremiah died. Although we now have added a new dog, Jasmine, to our family, Ruby now has claimed the spot permanently, even when the computer is not on.

My parents, Joan and Rod Wells, have helped in important ways. They have served as important role models and always supported my academic pursuits. While working on the dissertation, my father's constant eagerness to set a date to fly out for graduation kept me moving along. As my motivation sometimes ebbed, these reminders were quite helpful. He passed away a year after I finished; so I am certainly thankful for his persistence.

My mother grew up in a working class family and was the first one in her family to go on to college. She even completed a master's degree in education, which was when she met my father. Like many middle class wives (perhaps especially ones that grew up in working class homes), she was a full-time homemaker, while my brother and I were growing up. In her mid-forties she became actively involved in the labor force doing nonprofit community work. Since entering wage work, she has become a community leader and has expressed puzzlement at how she managed all those years as 'just a housewife.' As you read on, you will discover my answer to that puzzle.

While not on the title page I do wish to thank Earlham College, where I taught prior to coming to Arizona State, for its assistance. Special gratitude goes to Elaine Nelson, the interlibrary loan librarian, and the computer staff for helping provide me the resources and tools to research and write revisions to the manuscript.

Finally, I would like to thank the folks at Ashgate for giving me the opportunity to present this book to a wider audience.

David R. Wells
Tempe, Arizona

Introduction

Today we truly live in a world of goods. So much so that we nearly take it for granted. Shopping has become a favorite social activity and an activity that is often gender-typed as feminine. Yet what is the link between consumerism, capitalism and gender?

Within popular culture, modern consumerism is generally thought to be a phenomenon of the post-World War II era. Certainly in contrast to the Great Depression that idea seems true. Yet actually historians trace the roots of consumerism back to the sixteenth century (McKendrick 1982), although the particular escalation in material values appears to hasten in the late nineteenth century with the rise of monopoly capitalism.

In the vernacular, our understanding of consumerism has often been framed in terms of manipulative advertising at one extreme or the accelerated pace of technical progress meeting human needs at the other. What is intriguing is that neither of these explanations has a particular gender emphasis to them. This suggests that popular explanations are at best incomplete.

Academic research on consumerism has often emphasized its class nature or its gender nature. An integration of these two themes has generally been incomplete. Two examples demonstrate this point. Even though Thorstein Veblen's *Theory of the Leisure Class* noted how wealthy men placed their adorned wives on conspicuous display, his emphasis was on social class, not gender. Conversely, Susan Porter Benson in her book, *Countercultures: Saleswomen, Managers, and Customers in American Department Stores, 1890-1940* notes that department stores primarily served upper class women. However, she does not fully explore the class meaning and roots of consumption.

I do not merely wish to connect class and gender to the development of consumerism. I will argue that consumerism, although a key element in the successful establishment of the homemaker ideal, ultimately undermines it and becomes a motivating force (although not the only one) for why middle and upper class women moved from homemakers to the work force in the twentieth century. In a reversal of ideals, we now see that homemaking is no longer a position of high prestige for women, but actually one that may invite social scorn, especially the single or divorced mother who relies on state assistance to help her raise her children.

In the first two chapters of the book I argue that we need a theory of consumption in order to understand why women entered the labor force. In chapter one, I review the empirical data since 1890 on married women's labor force participation. Although early census figures understate the actual level of participation, I see a general growth especially among urban white married women. However, this growth in wage work I argue initially is largely tied to social class with working class women being far more likely to be engaged in paid labor. Not until 1960 do we see a trend suggesting that middle and upper class women are doing the same. The fact that monetary 'need' is so strongly correlated with labor force participation, even though through much of the period male wages are rising suggests a possible underlying consumer motivation, co-existing with a homemaker ideal. However, after 1960 that ideal appears to be in decline.

These dual issues of working for wages, as opposed to working in the home, suggest the need for a theoretical understanding of how the division of labor in the home is determined. In chapter two I examine neoclassical and Marxist-Feminist arguments regarding the division of labor, noting that the former is based on biological determinism and the latter subjugates gender issues to class. Patriarchy as an alternative to these approaches often is taken as a persistent form of domination. Gender-creating processes instead must be seen as dynamic. They can be both reproduced and challenged through the social structure of capitalism. With respect to consumerism, what is missing in these analyses is an examination of social value: how the social values of the market (consumerism) come to supersede the social values created by a woman at home (homemaking).

In chapter three I answer the first part of that question by examining how the social relations of capitalism (without gender) promote consumerism in a way other social formations that preceded capitalism do not. I attach particular importance to greater nominal class mobility in capitalism, urbanization which spreads contact with others but at a superficial level, the loss of labor-leisure choice by workers, and a growing individualism in the culture. Consumerism becomes a means of social expression for maintaining a person's sense of self-worth in a way that does not threaten the ruling classes.

Concern with capitalist work relations probably started with Adam Smith and his concerns with the 'stupefying' aspects of an extreme division of labor. Capitalist work processes represented a drastic change in the configuration of work. In pre-capitalist modes, the worker had a strong connection between his or her labor and the sustenance of his or her labor power. Most work was agricultural and done at the time and choice of the family with the obvious constraints of obtaining an adequate food supply in the context of seasonal weather changes. Even the early division of labor with the formation of craftsmen, while a bit less connected to direct survival, permitted the close proximity of crafts people to agriculture and, thus, allowed work and survival to form a coherent whole.

As urbanization spreads, work and survival lose this coherence as greater and greater division of labor leads to the growing distinction between work and survival. No longer does the worker consume his work. Workers do not even own their work, rather their pay is dictated by the hope that enough people will desire their product that they can receive enough in a common currency (money) to then pay others for the direct means of their livelihood. This tremendous change leaves the worker adrift, seeking definition.

Within chapter three, I detail a theory of consumption along these lines, but something is missing here which points to why the omission of gender is critically important. If the preceding story were correct, then why is shopping generally considered a feminine rather than a masculine activity? Although men were the people primarily experiencing capitalist social relations, women generally often worked under less formally capitalist conditions as domestic servants or escaped paid work entirely. Like pre-capitalist modes, within the home women produce the very products that are consumed. Hence, women do not appear to share the same consumption motives as men. Likewise, considering women mere functionaries of male prerogatives for material consumption is also inadequate.

In chapter four I suggest that gender is not only important in understanding the rise of mass consumption society, but also in why women entered the capitalist work place. Chapter four develops the reasons for both the rise of a homemaker ideal as well as its fall. It adds gender to the theory of consumption by noting that although wealthy men worked long hours in labor markets for substantial pay, they did not have time to shop. However, their wives with domestics doing all the hard work certainly did. The first department stores, truly palaces of consumption, in the late nineteenth century catered to wealthy women – the very women for whom a homemaker ideal was becoming the new social norm.

Homemaking was often defined in material consumption terms. In large part I argue that status differentials were critical in the creation of the homemaker ideal and their disappearance necessary for its demise. That demise was correlated with how consumerism changed relations of production within housekeeping. The homemaker ideal was both structurally dependent on wealthier women exploiting other women – domestic servants – as well as increasingly transformed into an activity that required higher consumption in order to propagate itself. The precipitous decline of domestic servants and proliferation of appliances after World War II shake the foundations of homemaking status differentials leading to its decline.

Chapter five more fully brings patriarchy into the analysis by examining the dynamics within households leading women to the labor market. Women found that through wage work, they could acquire greater relative power within the home. The fact that power becomes somewhat equated with money-earning also relates to the changed social values regarding consumerism. However, clear class differences also emerge. With the decline of the homemaker ideal, working class wives were more often motivated by monetary reasons for working than their middle and upper class counterparts. Middle and upper class wives were motivated by reasons related to ego satisfaction and a divergence between their actual marital power and their ideological beliefs supposed shared by their husbands regarding the dispersion of marital power. Ironically, through outside work, working class women due to their greater relative monetary contribution by some measures gain more relative power within marriage than their middle class counterparts. Yet in either case, wage work became a means to the twin ends of higher living and greater marital power.

The conclusion looks at the wider picture, as another change that has occurred this century is the decline in the married couple household itself. Thus, to just look at dynamics within these households, ignores an increasingly large number of families. Women here fare far worse economically, but often the problems resulting from tensions between consumerism and patriarchy placed them there in the first place.

1 Empirical research on married women's employment

Introduction

The labor force activity of married women has continually been connected to their level of income adequacy. Jacob Mincer's (1962) pioneering study empirically demonstrated that women do work for the money in the sense that, if their wage is higher, their labor force participation increases. Such a statement may seem obvious to a contemporary observer only because we take for granted the decision-making process which emphasizes income level in determining what kind of labor one will engage in. We presume the set of social values that can be summarized in the concept 'consumerism.' Due to a patriarchal division of labor which pervades both the work place and the home, most married women are secondary income earners, if they are employed at all. Thus, changes in the allocation of their time indicate changing social value systems and/or changing macroeconomic conditions.

The growth of consumerism is critical in understanding why married women are no longer exclusively housebound. In historical comparison, virtually all husbands provide substantially greater resources for their wives today than husbands provided for their wives in the very early years of the twentieth century. Thus, changed social values must influence the behavior of many married women.

The predominant social value system is consumerism. By consumerism I mean that capitalist commodities have an essential meaning for how we see ourselves in society and how we view others. The rise of consumerism results from more public modes of provision. Consumerism follows from the shift from domestic-centered provision to market-centered provision. One's own labors are increasingly separated from consumption. Thus, one must re-enter the social arena of exchange in order to choose one's subsistence and thereby engage in market transactions to procure use-values (Lebowitz 1982). But by making use-value procurement more social, the nature of the use-values has changed. The use-values become much more socially determined, and through this process become more than functional use-values – as they also carry self-identity.[1]

The fact that a particular persona is suggested by wearing 'Calvin Klein' underwear implies an internalization of values such that even very private consumption still carries socially determined status. Even though no one except perhaps a significant other (who already knows you) will see it indicates that the commodity has social value even when it is not displayed to others. In some cases the commodity empowers the owner to display new personalities that would otherwise be dormant. Hence, under consumerism one cannot conceive of oneself independent of capitalist produced commodities. They are critical in defining oneself to others as well as providing self-esteem. To rob someone of their commodities is to leave them barren. In fact, psychological research has established this very result (Belk 1988). Yet consumerism develops out of a social, historical process.

In the next two chapters, I note how consumerism is embedded in analyses of women's labor forced participation, but not overtly developed. Chapter one focuses on empirical work. The first part of the chapter is designed to provide an accurate measure of just how many married women were engaged in wage work since 1890. Prior to 1940 patriarchal ideology often led to the significant under counting of women's labor activities. The second part of the chapter examines the correlation between husband's income, female wages, and education levels in determining whether wives engage in wage work. The chief finding is that especially since the early twentieth century, a lack of income relative to other families has been a driving force in women's wage work decisions, but that since the 1960s that relationship has become less clear.

I will focus on white, urban married women in the following analysis, since contained within them are the upper class who represent the behavioral 'ideal' that other whites may attempt to emulate. In general, I assume consumption motives to be at best identical for women of color, but more likely to be muted due to pervasive discrimination that lowered their ability to use consumption goods as a means of lowering degrees of social stratification. However, I do not explore this hypothesis. Hence, although in this chapter I will sometimes refer to racial differences, their primary purpose is to illustrate the extremes of social stratification.

Urban behavior is the second focus. Although consumerism has come to envelope the entire country, urban areas were its genesis. Many of the arguments in chapter three concerning the display impact of consumption are strongly related to the broader more superficial social connections that develop with urbanization.

Estimating married urban white women's labor force participation: 1890-1930

The extent of change can be seen especially in the last fifty years. Whereas in 1940 only 14 percent of married women were in the labor force, today more than 60 percent are. These women have increasingly moved from being full-time housewives to full-time and part-time wage earners. As a result, the monetary output of a wife's labor has increased relative to her husband's income.

When families were primarily agricultural both husbands and wives produced essential materials for family reproduction. The absence of a market valuation for these labors makes it apparent that both labors were necessary for survival. The fact that family work was closely tied to family consumption meant that families did not have extra labor which they could send to a capitalist labor market. In fact, not until children became young adults might a surplus of labor emerge. The first textile workers in early nineteenth century New England were single women from farms – extra labor.

However, with industrial growth and urbanization, male labors were increasingly moved toward the market, while many female activities remained within the home. This separation reinforced the patriarchal division of labor (Humphries 1993). Thus, the labor market participation of married white women was considerably below their husbands. Table 1.1 gives a brief rundown of the number of married women actively involved in the labor force.

Although Table 1.1 presents census data, the figures do not always represent an accurate count of women's labor force activities. As early as 1870 the census sought to exclude the labors of women who did not earn a monetary remuneration. They did not make the same distinction for men until 1910. But even then much more latitude was given as gainfully employed could equal receiving a money income or a monetary equivalent for any work tied to the production of market goods (Folbre and Abel 1989).

Even when women did earn income, it was not always included. Census counters were known to exclude some occupations of women, particularly boardinghouse keepers and farm laborers. The 1890 census included the following instructions for counting employed women:

Table 1.1
Percent of married women in the labor force, 1890-1990 (all races)

1890	1900	1910	1920	1930	1940	1950	1960	1970	1980	1990
4.6	5.6	10.7	9.0	11.7	13.8	21.6	30.6	39.5	50.1	58.4
6.2	8.7	10.7	---	---	---	---	---	---	---	---

Sources: First Row: 1890-1980: Census data from Goldin (1990,p. 17). 1990: Current Population Survey data U.S. Dept. of Commerce. Bureau of Census (1993,p. 399). Second Row: Estimates of 1890 and 1900 based on 1910 reporting methods by Geib-Gunderson (1995, Table 4).

> For a woman who works only occasionally or for a short-time each day at outdoor or garden work, or in the dairy, or in the caring of livestock or poultry, the return shall be none. (quoted in Jenson 1980,p. 14)

Goldin (1979) found from population census data that in 1880 14 percent of white households in Philadelphia had boarders, yet the 1880 census noted that fewer than 1 percent of dwellings in Philadelphia had a boardinghouse keeper. This was not surprising, given typical instructions as found in the 1920 census. Taking in boarders and lodgers:

> should be returned as an occupation only if engaged in it and relies upon it as his (or her) principal means of support or principal source of income... If, however, a family keeps a few boarders or roomers merely as a means of supplementing or eking out the earnings of income obtained from other occupations or other sources, no one in the family should be returned as boarding or lodging housekeeper. (quoted in Jenson 1980,p. 15)

By contrast, the 1910 census actively encouraged the counting of women engaged in income-producing farm activities. Census workers were asked to report women working, even if as unpaid family workers. Consequently, the number of gainfully employed women went up. The number of women officially counted as engaged in agriculture increased from 3.3 to 5.2 percent from 1900 to 1910, even though the number of women on farms continued to decline (Wandersee 1981). However, the improved counting was not consistently followed, as the improvements were concentrated in the southern cotton producing states only (Goldin 1990). For this reason, economic historian Claudia Goldin's *Understanding the Gender Gap* (1990) disregards the 1910 census for examining trends, but uses it for purposes of estimating how many women would be counted as working by the definition of labor force participation used since 1940. Likewise, Lisa Geib-Gunderson (1995) uses the Public Use Microdata Sample (PUMS) for 1910 to determine the likelihood of women being counted as gainfully employed and estimated a 50 percent increase in employment levels had the same counting techniques been used in 1890 and 1900 as in 1910 (see Table 1.1 second row).

Hence, census figures prior to 1940 may not be reliable. Like the 1910 census stands out as particularly inconsistent with the other pre-1940 census figures, the 1930 census also may have had a comparatively more liberal accounting of female labor (Smuts 1960). In general, the census figures from 1890-1900 and 1920-1930 are roughly consistent in the methodology they employed and their tendency to under count the labor force activity of women, especially married women.

To establish a more accurate estimation of the urban married female work force, two areas of inconsistency must be addressed: the changed definition of 'gainful' employment to 'labor force' participant and the systematic under counting of women's labor force activities in the informal sector such as boardinghouse keepers.

Beginning in 1940, census figures switched from 'gainful' employment to 'labor force' participant. The labor force definition includes anyone as employed if *during the survey week* they worked at all for pay or worked at least 15 hours in unpaid family labor (for a family business, not housework) and then adds to that those unemployed and actively searching for work. By contrast the gainful worker definition is based on an accepted norm of days or weeks worked during the year. If a worker meets or exceeds that norm then the worker is counted as gainfully employed; if the person falls short then the person is not counted.

Goldin uses historical data on the distribution of working women and finds that although the measurements are qualitatively different, meaning that different workers might be counted as employed under the systems, the overall percentage of employed women is not significantly impacted through 1910 (she does not attempt later comparisons).

Under the labor force construct, one's probability of being counted as employed is based on the percent of days out of the general maximum which one works. Goldin notes that the 1907 *Report on Condition of Women and Child Wage-Earners* (U.S. Senate 1910-11), hereafter the 1907 Report, found that the average for single women workers older than 15 years of age was 249 days. If 300 represents the maximum number of days worked per year (roughly 6 days a week), then approximately 83 percent (249/300) of these women would be counted as employed during any given week if their weeks of work were randomly distributed.

By contrast, the gainful worker estimate depends on the societal norm and the distribution of working days. Using the 1907 Report, Goldin finds that if 150 days were the norm (or cut-off minimum for inclusion), 92 percent of the women would be counted. If 200 days were the norm, 83 percent would be counted. Thus, the two measures roughly coincide at 200 days.

The 1907 Report also included data on married women. They worked on average 212 days or 71 percent of the 300 possible days per year. The labor force estimate is, therefore, 71 percent. If the norm for a working day were 150 days then 73 percent would be counted as gainfully employed and at a norm of 175 days, 71 percent would be counted. Thus, the gainful worker and labor force participant measures of employed women coalesce at 175 days. The low drop with the increment of 25 days to the norm indicates the tightness of the distribution of days worked around the average.

Unfortunately, we do not know what norms were used by census takers. However, Goldin considers her sample norms reasonable given the intermittent nature of labor contracts during this time. Thus, if 150 were the norm, the gainful worker estimate is only slightly higher than labor force numbers and almost identical when the sample is restricted to married women. However, this coalescence may not always be the case. A survey comparing the 1930 and 1940 categorization of women found a 2.7 percent over count in 1930 due to the gainful worker definition (Durand 1968 [1948]). Thus, I will assume that in 1890 the gainful worker and labor force coalesce, but that by 1930 the gainful worker definition represented an approximately 25 percent over count.

The second area of correction regards the labor activities of women that were restricted to their homes. While boardinghouse keeping is not the only activity, as some women may have been engaged in piecework or taking in laundry, the under counting was primarily an issue of boardinghouse keeping perhaps because their labor represented an elongation of the homemaking activities already involved in taking care of their families. Although the extent of boarding is not known precisely prior to 1930, when the census first tracked the phenomena, most regional studies found 14 to 25 percent in various city populations. As noted earlier, Goldin used census data to determine a 14 percent figure for Philadelphia circa 1880. Modell and Hareven (1973) found in the Northeast cities of 1890 that boarding was approximately 15 percent.

Twenty-three percent of all husband-wife families in industrial communities surveyed in the 1890/91 report (U.S. Bureau of Labor 1892) had at least one boarder or non-nuclear family member with 16 percent (70 percent of the 23 percent) receiving income from boarders. The 1890/91 Report found average income from boarding at $201 per year.

Goldin's research suggests boarders occupied space that would have otherwise gone vacant, but that boarding families spent larger amounts on food, meaning that net income from boarding was approximately $140 per year, roughly 47 percent of the full-time income of women in the same regions.

If one attempts to apply the gainful worker concept to these boardinghouse keepers, Goldin suggests two alternatives. Due to a lack of hourly information on boardinghouse keeping, both alternatives are wage-based. She assumes that if wages were identical in manufacturing and boardinghouse keeping, then reported money earnings can be used to approximate time spent. Her first method includes only those boardinghouse keepers who earned at least half of the full-time income of a manufacturing worker – one interpretation of the gainful employment threshold. By this criterion 37 percent of boardinghouse keepers should be included.

The second method is based on the current labor force criterion for nonpaid family labor. Since boardinghouse keeping was a family business, the current labor force definition includes home workers if they work 37.5 percent of a normal work week (15/40). By applying that criterion to earnings (37.5 percent of full-time earnings), 46 percent would be included.

The final revision would be to include all boardinghouse keepers because the above measures discriminate on the basis of pay, not on the basis of days worked, which, if home-based work pays less, would be significantly more. By this measure all boardinghouse keepers are included. In Table 1.2, I have presented Goldin's estimated correction for the 1890 census.

In the years prior to the Depression, boarding dwindled as a social practice. Boarding was most common in growing urban areas. Urban migration from rural areas or foreign countries was highly correlated with boarding due to housing shortages. Taking on boarders to supplement income was also a function of class, with working class individuals being more likely to take on boarders, especially by the twentieth century. Modell and Hareven (1973) find evidence which suggest foreign-born families were no more likely to board than native ones, despite popular perceptions to the contrary. In addition, excluding boarders, the rooms per person in boarding households were greater than nonboarding households, somewhat undermining the overcrowding notion associated with boarding. The greater room figures, along with studies of who accepted boarders, indicate that middle-aged and older households were most likely have boarders. Boarders generally rented rooms that had been occupied by now grown children.

Table 1.2
Adjusted 1890 married women's employment rates

1890 Official Census Figure for Married Women: 4.6%

	A	B
Boardinghouse keepers:		
urban areas > 25,000 pop.	+1.3	+2.7
all non-farm < 25,000 pop.	+2.7	+5.9
Unpaid Agricultural Labor:		
cotton farms	+1.3	+1.3
other farms	+5.4	+5.4
Total adjustment	+10.7	+15.3
Adjusted figure	15.1%	19.2%

A: Counting 46% of boardinghouse keepers as labor force participants, as a good comparison with labor force figures.

B: Includes all boardinghouse keepers. Good estimate of how many married women earned money for their families.

Source: Goldin (1990,pp. 44, 222-227, 259-262).

Thus, boarding represented an escape hatch by which families earned money but were able to maintain a housebound wife. During the 1920s, studies in California and Chicago documented the economic relation of boarding. In California 11 percent of skilled typographers' homes and 22 percent of semi-skilled streetcar workers' homes had boarders, respectively. Twenty-eight percent of native white small wage earners in Chicago had boarders (Strasser 1982).

However, boarding declined with greater affluence, a decrease both in urban migration and foreign immigration, more housing and a continued public outcry against boarding. The percent boarding in urban areas in 1930 according to Census figures was 11.4 percent. During the depression era when migration was well down, but income needs higher than before, boarding continued to stumble. Census figures found for 1940 that boarding in urban areas was 9 percent, a 20 percent drop from 1930 (Modell and Hareven 1973).

Table 1.3
Employment rates for white and non-white married women

Year	All women	White	Non-white
1890	4.6%	2.6%	22.5%
1900	5.6	3.2	26.0
1910	Omitted	---	---
1920	9.0	6.5	32.5
1930	11.7	9.8	33.2

Source: Goldin (1990,p. 17 – Table 2.1) based on Census data.

Table 1.4
Estimates of white non-farm married women's labor force participation and money earning activities: 1890 and 1930
(in percent)

1890	Cities	Towns	All urban
Adjusted Census	3.9	3.9	3.9
+Boarding	7.4 (16.0)	4.9 (10.6)	6.5 (14.1)
Total	11.3 (19.9)	8.8 (14.5)	10.4 (18.0)

1930	Cities	Towns	All urban
Adjusted Census	10.2	10.2	10.2
+Boarding	4.7 (12.7)	3.1 (8.5)	4.2 (11.4)
Total	15.1 (24.1)	13.3 (20.3)	14.4 (23.0)

Figures in parentheses denote percent of *all* married white women earning income.

Cities are defined as having population greater than 25,000, while Towns had less than 25,000.

See Appendix for estimation details.

Sources: Vanek (1973,p. 9 – Table 1.5) based on Census data, Modell and Hareven (1973), Goldin (1990,pp. 222-227, 259-262) based on 1890/91 report, and Durand (1968 [1948]).

Besides correcting for boardinghouse keepers, an additional adjustment to census figures is needed to correct for race and residence. Both are problematic for a study of the effect of consumerism on women's labor force participation. The pressures of consumerism are most likely greatest in urban areas which were the centers of the new consumer culture. In addition, race adds another intervening variable which stands apart from the integration of patriarchy and capitalism which I am focusing on. Thus, I would like to develop an index of urban married white women's labor force participation. Race certainly mattered as non-white women (predominately African-American) were much more likely to be gainfully employed than white women (see Table 1.3).

The number of white married women in 1890 was approximately 10 million (Durand 1968 [1948]). Approximately 4 million of these women were on farms. However, only 23,000 of them were counted as gainfully employed as unpaid family workers or 0.6 percent (Smuts 1960). By algebra of the remaining 6 million white married women not living on farms, 3.9 percent were counted as gainfully employed. Assuming being counted did not vary between non-farm areas of different size populations, then we can readjust Goldin's estimates to determine an approximate married white female labor force participation rate for 1890 and an estimate of the percent of all white married females earning money income in 1890. Making similar assumptions, we can estimate the actual labor force participation for married white women in 1930, taking into account declining boardinghouse keeping and an over count relative to 1940. Table 1.4 presents these estimates and indicates a 20 percent growth in money earning activities with formal labor force activity replacing boardinghouse keeping. However, the increase is 40 percent, if only those defined as labor force participant are considered.

Possible explanations for married white women entering the labor force

Three explanations are frequently put forward to suggest why married women's labor force participation increased in the early twentieth century: lost income from boarding and child labor, greater job opportunities due to higher female education and an expanded demand for clerical jobs, and lower female fertility rates along with higher life expectancy. While each of these appear reasonable, they fail to provide compelling explanations for the rising labor force participation rate where it was occurring the greatest: younger working class women.

Lost supplemental income

The loss of boarding income was described above, yet the loss of boarding income was not the only change facing working class families. Urban families lost another secondary source of income, child labor. After 1910, child labor laws were passed and the number of children graduating from high school began to increase dramatically.

As a result, the number of children engaged in paid labor between age 10 and 17 fell significantly. This can be seen in Tables 1.5 and 1.6. Although census data did not count all of the jobs children might take to earn income, it does provide some semblance of the trend of the extent child labor was available (Wandersee 1981).

These declining sources of supplemental income streams would seem to be an obvious reason for heightened married white women's labor force participation, but a cohort analysis suggests that consumerism may be a more important explanation. Goldin (1991) and Oppenheimer (1970) point to this restriction in supply of other workers along with the expansion of clerical opportunities as a demand pull for married women into the labor market beginning in the 1920s. However, a closer look at participation rates reveals an underlying social change, reflecting a heightened need for monetary income among younger married women.

Although middle-aged and older families suffered the greatest loss of income from boarding and child labor, younger married women aged 25-34 were just as likely to enter the labor market as those aged 45-54. Older families were more likely to have children in the labor force or to have had the extra space for boarders since their children had left home. In fact, Modell and Hareven (1973) found families with a male head aged 45 and older to be three and a half times more likely to have boarders than those with a male head aged 25-44. However, between 1920 and 1930, the labor force participation rate increases by more for women aged 25-34 than it does for those aged 45-54. This same cohort, aged 25-34 in 1920, increases its labor force participation dramatically when they reach 45-54 in 1950, becoming the first (in terms of birth year) to ever eclipse the 20 percent labor force participation rate (see Table 1.7). This suggests a broader social change influencing labor force participation. This broader change is also suggested by the fact that in 1950, married women of all ages show significant increases in the number engaged in wage work. The cohort born in 1896-1905 is a transitional cohort, as its increases in labor force participation before 1950 signal the broader increases which follow.

Table 1.5
Percentage of children 10-15 years old of both sexes in the labor force, 1880-1930

Year	% Total Children	% Male Children	% Female Children
1880	16.8	24.4	9.0
1890	18.1	25.9	10.0
1900	18.2	26.1	10.2
1910	18.4	24.8	11.9
1920	8.5	11.3	5.6
1930	4.7	6.4	2.9

Source: Wandersee (1981,p. 61 – Table 3.2) from 1930 Census data.

Table 1.6
Percentage of children 14-19 years old of both sexes in the labor force, 1900-1940

Age	1900	1910	1920	1930	1940
14-15	30.9	30.7	17.5	9.2	5.2
Male	43.4	41.4	23.3	12.6	8.0
Female	18.2	19.8	11.6	5.8	2.2
16-17	---	---	44.7	31.7	21.0
Male	---	---	58.0	41.2	29.0
Female	---	---	31.6	22.1	12.9
18-19	---	---	60.0	55.3	52.7
Male	---	---	78.3	70.7	65.6
Female	---	---	42.3	40.5	40.5

Source: Wandersee (1981,p. 62 – Table 3.3) from 1940 Census data.

Table 1.7
Labor force participation for married white women by cohort and cross section

		Age			
	Birth year	15-24	25-34	35-44	45-54
	1866-1875	2.9	3.1	4.7[a]	5.9[b]
	1876-1885	3.0	5.4[a]	6.3	7.8
By cohort	1886-1895	5.6[a]	7.7	9.8	10.1
	1896-1905	**8.2**	**11.5**	**13.8**	**22.2**
	1906-1915	13.3	16.7	25.3	38.6
	1916-1925	14.7	21.0	35.4	46.7

		Age			
	Calendar year	15-24	25-34	35-44	45-54
	1890	2.9	2.6	2.5	2.3
	1900	3.0	3.1	3.1	2.6
	1910	5.6[a]	5.4[a]	4.7[a]	4.3[a]
By cross section	1920	**8.2**	7.7	6.3	5.9[b]
	1930	13.3	**11.5**	9.8	7.8
	1940	14.7	16.7	**13.8**	10.1
	1950	24.9	21.0	25.3	**22.2**

[a] Due to 1910 inconsistency, the average of 1900 and 1920 census for same age group is taken.
[b] In 1920 age 45-54 was grouped with 55-64. I have split the figures based on a weighted average of 1/3 of the difference between these age groups in 1900 and 2/3 of the difference in 1930.

Source: Goldin (1990,p. 18) based on Census data.

Table 1.8
Median education for married white women, 1890 and 1930

Year	Age				
	15-24	25-34	35-44	45-54	55-64
1890	7.8*	<8	<8	<8	<8
1930	10.8	**9**	8.2	8	7.8*

* Same cohort.
1896-1905 cohort is in **bold**.
<8 Precise figures unavailable, may be significantly less than 8.

Source: Goldin (1990,p. 145).

Table 1.9
High school graduation rates by race

Birth Year	High School Grad. Year	White Grad. Rate	10 yr. % Rise	Non-white Grad. Rate	10 yr. % Rise
1870	1887	15%	---	5%	---
1880	1897	20	33%	6	20%
1890	1907	25	25	7	17
1900	**1917***	**30**	**20**	**10**	**43**
1910	1927*	45	50*	18	80*

Birth year of 1900 in the 1896-1905 cohort is in **bold**.
* Post child labor restrictions.

Source: Goldin (1990,p. 144).

Increased educational attainment

The rise in younger cohorts working could have two other explanations: increased educational attainment and falling fertility rates. However, neither explanation is sufficient unless one adds social class and the rise of consumerism. Table 1.8 suggests the increasing role of education in women's labor force participation. The rise in clerical and professional occupational areas from 1890 to 1930 from 13.6 percent of women workers to 37.4 percent is indicative of the impact higher education levels had on work choices. Although these figures are for all working women, given the shrinking work span for women prior to marriage due to higher years spent in education, it seems plausible to surmise that this trend carried over to married women as well and formed the basis of some women choosing careers.

Yet, while some highly educated women did enter the work force, the great increase coming from the 1896-1905 cohort actually represents the beginning of education trickling down to the lowest social classes. While education levels by white social class are not available, they are separated by race. If we can infer that blacks in the aggregate corresponded in economic terms to the lowest quartile of whites, then beginning around 1920, there may have been a significant increase in the education of working class white women (see Table 1.9).

Due to non-whites' much higher labor participation rates – often beginning at an early age – the graduation rates might understate the spread of education to lower white social classes. However, if we compare the relative increases in the graduation rates after child labor laws became more restrictive (* years in Table 1.9), we note the qualitative shift towards higher graduation rates improvement both among whites and non-whites. With their improved education levels after the enactment of child labor laws correlating with a cohort which significantly increased its labor force participation rate, working class white women appear to be the ones most actively moving into the labor force. In fact, the period 1916-1940 corresponds with the transcendence of secondary schooling to a mass institution (Walters and Rubinson 1983). By 1930 the first effects of this change might be seen. Thus, education itself is not a cause of working, except when viewed through class access. Particular women engaged in wage work – those in the lower 50 percent of whites. Those among the top 20 percent were the first to attain high graduation rates, but this did not greatly change their likelihood to engage in wage work. These wealthier women had a choice between money-earning labor and a combination of homework and leisure (homework being limited by servant help), since the income of their husbands enabled them to live on his 'family wage'. However, for poorer families the issue of consumerism and inadequate husband support, made giving up the prospect of a wife's income more problematic; so, many of them opted for wage work. The relationship between consumerism, a homemaker ideology and women's work will be developed in chapters four and five.

Declining fertility rates

A contributing factor no doubt was not just the availability of better jobs, but also general decreases in fertility rates and infant mortality. However, we note a significant lag between falling fertility and white women entering the labor force in large numbers. For women aged 15-44 during the nineteenth century, fertility rates fell by more than fifty percent from 280 to 130 births per thousand. After 1900, the rate of decrease diminishes until the depression years when the rate plummets by another third (U.S. Dept. of Commerce 1975). Then, during the early post-World War II decades, we see a rise in fertility to 1920 levels at the same time as women are entering the workforce in large numbers. Hence, the aggregate data does seem to support a direct link between lower fertility and women's labor force participation.

Surely the lower rates of fertility were a necessary prerequisite for women entering the labor market, especially younger working class women. While the following is with reference to Britain, the situation in the United States would not be significantly different:

> It would be probably true to say that at the beginning of the [twentieth] century about half of all working wives over the age of forty had borne between seven and fifteen children ... it would seem that the typical working class mother of the 1890's, married in her teens or early twenties and experiencing about ten pregnancies, spent about fifteen years in a state of pregnancy and in nursing a child for the first year of its life ... the expectation of life of a woman aged twenty was forty-six years. Approximately one-third of this life expectancy was to be devoted to the physiological and emotional experience of childbearing and maternal care in infancy. Today the expectation of life of a woman aged twenty is fifty-five years. Of this longer expectation only about 7 percent of the years to be lived will be concerned with childbearing and maternal care in infancy. (Titmus 1963,pp. 90-91)

Urbanization had particularly depressing effects on birthrates. In large part this appears to be due to the lessened economic value of children in cities compared to farms and the degree of economic need itself. Immigrants and blacks representing two of the poorer groups in society had substantially higher fertility rates. Fertility rates tended to fall first among the wealthier native whites during the nineteenth century, with the native white working class following a generation later but still reaching fairly low levels in the late nineteenth century, approximately one birth for every ten women aged 15-44 each year. Rural white, immigrant white and African-American women were still approaching these levels at the onset of the Great Depression (Van Horn 1986, Easterlin 1968). Thus, the most likely hypothesis is that younger working class women took the extra time afforded them through better health care, higher education, and falling fertility to move into the labor market, while the upper and middle class women who experienced these changes up to a generation earlier continued to stay home.

Family income

Family income outside of the wife's contribution then becomes the dominant predictor of married women's labor force participation. An astute economist would presumably argue that this is not surprising. Families had target real income levels and when their husbands were unable to reach those targets, wives engaged in a cost-benefit analysis in determining whether to stay home or enter the labor force. As the costs of leaving the home diminished, poorer wives would be predicted to enter the labor market. However, this apparently simple decision leaps over two important issues: an income target and the mechanics of cost-benefit analysis. In a society increasingly consumption-oriented, but also emphasizing a homemaker ideal for wives, this decision is actually very complex.

Empirical research on married women's labor force participation: 1950-1985

Empirical analyses during the post-World War II years suggest the continued motivation of rising living standards, but also a significant change in the behavior of wealthier women toward moving into the labor market. Hence, unlike the pre-war years where consumerism co-existed with a homemaker ideal, the post-war years suggest that consumerism supplants the homemaker ideal.

Econometric studies can be useful in disaggregating data to reflect how particular variables, independent of the effects of other variables, correlate

21

with labor force participation. The strong monetary impact reflected in econometric studies supports embedded consumerism. Generally, aside from the presence of young children, husband's income (negative) and wages for women and the wife's education (both positive) are some of the key effects determining whether women worked.

Jacob Mincer's (1962) pioneering work used 1949 aggregate cross section data from 57 Standard Metropolitan Statistical Areas (SMSAs). The dependent variable was married women's labor force participation. Significant results were found for husband's income (negative) and median income of women who worked 50-52 weeks (positive). In addition, he found support for a greater positive substitution effect (due to wife's income) over the negative income effect (due to husband's income).[2] The substitution effect is relevant in that it suggests to what degree married women are motivated by income reasons to work independent of 'need' as suggested by husband's income. Thus, the Mincer regression appeared to suggest a falling homemaker ideal.

The regression, however, did not reflect the experience of individual women, rather it represented aggregate differences across the means for the 57 urban areas studied. The flaw in this approach is the use of aggregate data to infer individual behavior (Fox 1980). However, Mincer's work was the first to attempt to isolate the income and substitution effects on women's labor force participation.

Mincer's efforts led other economists to examine 1960 data for the same effects. Glen Cain (1966) found that unlike 1950, in 1960 the husband's negative income effect exceeded the positive effect of rising women's earnings. Poorer women were more likely to engage in paid labor than wealthier women and the homemaker ideal may still have remained.

Similar results were found by William Bowen and T. Aldich Finegan (1969), but their research also raises the question of broader social changes beyond what purely economic variables can predict. Bowen and Finegan used the 1 in 1,000 sample data aggregated across SMSAs from the 1960 census as their primary data, but also sought to replicate the work of Mincer with 1940 and 1950 data. As such their data base was essentially similar to Cain. Like Cain, they found the husband's income effect less than the wife's substitution effect was true only for 1950 data. More troubling to them was that correcting for demographic changes from 1948-1965, that economic variables only 'explained' 4 percent of the actual change in women's labor force participation, 14.6 percent (see Table 1.10). They attributed much of the unexplained area to rising income aspirations, i.e. consumerism.

Table 1.10
Percent change in married women's labor force participation 1948-1965 'explained' by changes in economic variables

- 6.3%	increase in family non-wife income
+2.9	rise in women's education
- 0.7	decrease in husband's unemployment rate
+4.6	rise in women's wages
<u>+3.4</u>	<u>local industry mix – relative to female occupations</u>
+4.0%*	Total explained by economic factors

*does not exactly sum to 4.0 due to rounding errors.

Source: Bowen and Finegan (1969, p. 218).

Despite the fallacy of composition, aggregate data did attempt to measure the substitution effect. Since not all women were employed, using aggregate employed women's income data provided a possible measure of the general effect of rising female wages on married women's labor force participation. However, aggregate data cannot provide an adequate understanding of the economic motives leading individual women to seek work in the context of consumerism. Individual data would provide a better indicator of individual behavior.

James Sweet (1973) took such an approach using the 1 in 1,000 census data for 1960. He specifically sought to define a measure of income adequacy as an indicator of whether women worked. Using a 1959 New York City budget study for private agencies to determine whether families of various sizes qualified for assistance (Morgan, David, Cohen and Brazer 1962), Sweet constructed an income adequacy index from 0.0 - 0.3 to 2.9 and greater based on the husband's income. An income of 1 meant the husband's income equaled the assistance cut off for a family of his particular size, while an index of 3 would signify three times that level of income. With this measure and controlling for youngest child's age, number of children, and wife's age and education, Sweet demonstrated a significant negative correlation between income adequacy and whether the wife worked (for white women only).

Studies in the 1970s continued to find an inverse relation between a husband's income and whether his wife worked. One such example is a 1974-75 random sample of 2,248 respondents in the contiguous 48 states. Statistically significant individual results[3] were found for wife's education (positive), family life stage (presence and age of children, negative and decreasing), husband's income (negative) and husband's education (positive). In addition, they found a positive association with women working and their holding a nontraditional sex-role ideology. The strongest effects came from husband's income and family life-stage (Geerken and Grove 1983).

Lehrer and Nerlove (1980) used a more complex regression, relating wife's labor supply and fertility to husband's income, wife's education and other variables. Their individual data was derived from the 1973 National Survey of Family Growth. They also found a negative relationship between husband's income and the wife working. Their findings suggest, however, that the wife's education might have a stronger positive influence than the negative income effect of husband's income.

Although in the aggregate poorer husbands' wives may be more likely to be employed, when the increase in women's labor force participation is analyzed along a marginal basis, this no longer holds. Since 1960, the *increase* in participation rates has been relatively more concentrated among wives of middle and upper income husbands (Ryscavage 1979). In fact, the full effect could be seen in Rebecca Blank's (1988) analysis of the 1985 Current Population Survey where husbands of working wives had higher incomes than husbands of full-time housewives. This result suggests a departure from a patriarchal ideology which embraced homemaking. Thus, the post-1960 data suggests that rising income aspirations began to supersede the patriarchal ideology based on a housebound wife.

Chapters four and five will investigate how growing consumerism interacted with this patriarchal ideology.

Conclusion

The labor force participation rates of married urban white women has steadily increased since 1890. However, the pace of increase has risen tremendously in the years since the end of World War II. Analysis of the labor force participation of married women through the early 1970s shows a negative relationship between household income and the wife's work decision. However, since 1960, income may not be as significant a predictor of wives' work decisions.

Relative husband's income serving to motivate women's wage work is consistent with Duesenberry's (1949) relative income hypothesis of consumption. He asserted a demonstration effect for consumption, whereby people's desire to acquire consumption items is influenced by the consumption

24

patterns of others. Since lower income households have a greater difference between their actual consumption and that which is socially demonstrated, wives in these households have a greater impetus to work.

However, the fact that econometric studies under predict changes in wives' labor force participation suggests broader social changes occurring. These can reflect a growing materialism and individualism in society, leading women to place a greater incentive on income-earning activities. More weakly stated, it may merely reflect households seeking greater efficiency with their labors. As capitalist labor markets provide cheaper substitutes for home production, women change their labor allocation toward the capitalist labor market. The answer to these two possibilities will depend on how families with (wage) working wives spend their income compared to those with those families whose wives do not engage in wage work (see end of chapter four for this discussion).

While economists often leave the level of argument at this depth, they ignore the patriarchal (i.e., gender-based) use-values given up by having a wife work outside the home. Certainly these use-values are not an insignificant part of what delayed the entrance of wealthier husbands' wives into the labor force and acted as a restraint on working class wives as well. This homemaker ideal represented a social valuation of familial patriarchy. The attitude might best be seen in the following statement by a 39 year old married high school graduate with an eleven year old son in 1957:

> My son and I don't want her to work. We're spoiled. She does everything for us. I like her to prepare lunch for me. ... I said to her, 'What is the matter with you? Do you have a guilt complex about staying home? If I were after you to work that would be different, but I am not.' Oh I may be old fashioned. My mother never worked. Of course, most of the time I didn't need her, but when I needed her, she was right there. So I think it's all wrong for her to work, unless it's really necessary. I think during the last year or so she began to see things our way and is satisfied to stay home. (Komarovksy 1962,p. 61)

The patriarchal power relations impeding the wife's choice are obvious, as only what the husband judges as proper is allowable. Thus, the transition, from a condition where use-values associated with patriarchy are strong enough such that they limit competing use-values provided by the capitalist market to a condition where the capitalist market predominates, cannot be understood without addressing issues of gender and patriarchal control.

Notes

1. 'Use-value' or the usefulness of a product is in contrast to 'exchange-value' or the actual price of the product.

2. The income effect implies one buys more goods, including 'leisure', while the substitution effect suggests a higher wage means not working for pay ('leisure') is more expensive and will be sought less. The economists' use of 'leisure' is problematic when discussing the nonpaid activities women perform. However, the distinction between paid and nonpaid time is a valid one.

3. At the one percent level or better.

2   Structural theories for married women's employment

The previous chapter suggested an important interaction between how society valued what women did in the home with competing values to earn money and buy consumption goods. An important underlying issue is what determines the gender division of labor and what forces might lead women to move into the labor market. This chapter addresses how Marxist-Feminist and neoclassical perspectives have framed the issue of why women work. The two differ primarily in how they approach the role of patriarchy within the household in determining the sexual division of labor. This section principally presents a summary critique of the theoretical literature. The analysis will focus on the neoclassical perspective as represented by Gary Becker and debates within the Marxist-Feminist perspective, although related views from functional sociology and patriarchal perspectives will be included. Because the neoclassical view ignores the issue of power and social structure, it distorts the concept of efficiency upon which the theory is based. The Marxist-Feminist works represent an attempt to correct the subordination of patriarchy to capitalism within Marx's and Engels' analyses. However, although Marxist-Feminists attempt to include the household, they still fail to integrate capitalism and patriarchy in a way which enables us to understand how the use-values purchased in the market come to transcend the use-values produced by the wife and consumed by the family patriarch. While all the theories suggest an underlying income-earning motivation, none offers a satisfactory explanation of rising consumption aspirations.

Materialism and patriarchy – missing theoretical connections

The new home economics of Gary Becker

Gary Becker recently won the Nobel Prize in economics in part for extending economics into the realm of sociology – the family. Becker (1991) argues that the concept of efficiency can be effectively used to explain household behavior relating to the sexual division of labor and other family concerns, including marriage, divorce and fertility.

Patriarchal power is not instrumental to his analysis. Distribution issues relating not only to material goods, but how time is allocated are completely melded into the concept of efficiency. Power issues within the home are ignored. This fact probably explains his rejection of feminist perspectives. Despite the impressive length of Becker's bibliography to *Treatise on the Family* (1991), one can find only one citation (Boserup 1987), a critique of his earlier work, that could be classified as feminist. Thus, Becker's approach is best seen as seeking to extend the neoclassical framework to the family. In so doing, he exposes his analysis to the same weaknesses of neoclassical theory, namely the omission of power. The only kind of power that neoclassical economists recognize is market power – the power to disproportionately influence price and quantity in markets. Becker essentially places members of households within a perfectly competitive framework, where they have no market power within the home.[1]

Becker determines the sexual division of labor through this market power type argument. He asserts that women have a monopoly in childbearing and that this is positively associated with a comparative advantage in childrearing. Therefore, women's duties include children. Why this necessarily means they must also specialize in vacuuming, cooking, shopping, and laundry is not clear – for they have no link with childrearing other than they are located within the home where the child is located, but as Heidi Hartmann (1974) and much earlier Charlotte Perkins Gilman (1913, 1966) have noted this technically could be organized otherwise. Thus, the fact that women are separated from the labor market is tied to the social structure where the labor market is separated from the home.

Given this comparative advantage which women have, men then fill the remaining duties. This reasoning leads to some antipatriarchal logic. Since women are so important to the reproduction of society, women *hire* men as breadwinners because men earn more (Humphries and Rubery 1984). Women have an absolute advantage in childrearing, which leads to men having a comparative advantage in market work. But Becker has no basis to assert that men have an absolute advantage in market work. Thus, consider the following case:

Hours to perform a unit of 'work'

	Childrearing	Market
Wife	8	8
Husband	12	8.

Here the husband has a comparative advantage in market work, while the wife has a comparative (and absolute advantage) in childrearing. If someone must stay home with the children, it will be the wife, yet we can see that the implicit power within this relationship (even though both are better off) lies with the wife – she is the more efficient of the two.[2] From this initial difference, Becker then asserts that women go on to specialize in childrearing and household 'capital', while men specialize in market 'capital', such that men become more efficient in the market sphere and women more efficient in the childrearing sphere:

Hours to perform a unit of 'work'

	Childrearing	Market
Wife	6	8
Husband	12	6.

Now the husband may actually have developed an absolute advantage in market work. The differences would be even more pronounced if we assume time away from a childrearing or market work depreciates one's capabilities. This would especially affect the wife who does not engage in any market work, while less so alter the husband's capabilities, since presumably he would still spend time with his children.

Becker further argues for the relative stability of this arrangement based on a comparative advantage that same sex couples could not enjoy:

Since the biological natures of men and women differ, the assumption that the time of men and women are perfect substitutes even at a rate different than unity is not realistic. Indeed their times are complements in sexual enjoyment, the production of children, and possibly other commodities produced by the household. Complementarily implies that households with men and women are more efficient than households with only one sex. (1991,p. 39)

From this backdrop, Becker argues that since investments in skills begins from childhood, biological sex differences tend to be reinforced. Although biological qualities of individuals may vary within each sex, those aberrant individuals may not manifest themselves until adolescence. Thus, even though a small minority of girls may have a biological disposition for the market (i.e., comparative advantage) and a small minority of boys a biological disposition for housework (i.e., comparative advantage), 'in the face of no initial information to the contrary, the optimal strategy would be to invest mainly household capital in *all* girls and mainly market capital in *all* boys until any deviation from this norm is established' (1991,p. 40). The net effect of this optimal strategy is to further reduce 'abnormal' behavior by girls and boys.

Girls, since they anticipate marriage, have a further disincentive to invest in market capital. These factors lead women to have lower market capital and therefore lower marginal products in the market sector, leading to lower wages when they do work.

Obvious implications follow from this work. Women should have 'U' shaped labor market supply functions over their adult lives, with the periods of childrearing being times when they are most likely to withdraw from the labor market and then re-enter when the children are older or grown. The allocation is a matter of *choice* and households act as a unitary function to maximize their utility, because this allocates household resources most efficiently.

Whether women work for wages is dependent on the opportunity cost – what they give up in order to work. For a given level of wages, the opportunity cost is dependent on the state of household technology, time necessary for childrearing and preferences for leisure. As capitalism has expanded, household technology has improved. Likewise, decreased fertility and the development of mandatory schooling have lifted much of the childrearing burden from mothers. Thus, from an opportunity cost standpoint, the opportunity cost of leaving home has diminished.

Since money wages provide revenue which can buy the material products and services which the household desires, higher female wages will make it more possible for women to purchase goods or services formerly produced in the home, further lowering the opportunity cost. As real wages rise, two effects exist. On the one hand, the greater income leads to purchase of all goods including leisure. However since the leisure is time-intensive and time has become relatively more expensive, the substitution effect argues that it will be economized. Time intensive commodities such as leisure will be reduced. If goods can be substituted for time, then more goods and less time will be used (Owen 1971). Sometimes this substitution will remove output from the home like buying baked goods, but sometimes waiting and travel time savings will place it back in the home, such as men shaving themselves, rather than going to a barber.

The substitution effect of market work and the implication that household devices would require less time in the home, leading to women's labor force participation, are simplistic and inaccurate. As will be discussed in chapter four, little evidence exists to demonstrate that household equipment eased housework immediately, rather the hours of full-time housewives remained constant from the mid-1920s when the first studies were done through the mid-1960s, despite tremendous changes in technology. This paradox requires one to examine the neoclassical black box of household production. Second, budget studies have failed to demonstrate that increased labor force participation has led to the purchase of household related goods, i.e., substitutes for the wife's labor (Brown 1985, Strober 1977, Vickery 1979). More will be developed on this issue in chapter four.

To neoclassical economists whether women engage in wage work or not essentially becomes a cost-benefit analysis. However, within this cost-benefit approach is the underlying issue of preferences and why households do not choose more leisure with rising incomes, rather than more income and more consumption. The substitution effect predominates only if materialism is more important than time. I will address this issue in chapter three.

Yet there are two further problems with Becker's analysis. Becker's apparent insights into cost-benefit analysis run into the fundamental obstacle of why our society is patriarchal. If women are the ones with 'market power' within the marriage due to their ability to give birth, then why is the prestige and power within the social structure focused on men, rather than women?

While men may have physical strength advantages, women have been thought to be more caring. However, Becker does not base his husband breadwinner argument on the basis of physical strength. He argues that because each household member's consumption is greatest if the total income of the household is highest, even selfish members of the household have an incentive to behave appropriately. Ironically, as Paula England has noted, to accomplish this task the positive characteristics of women are attributed to men in the Becker model:

> Becker argues that even a selfish 'rotten' spouse or child will be induced to 'behave' because of the reinforcement mechanism set up by the altruist. This 'rotten kid' theorem doesn't hold without the assumption that the family member who is an altruist *also* controls the resources to be distributed (Ben-Porath 1982, Pollak 1985) ... Becker ignores male power and its potentially harmful effects on women while exaggerating male altruism. It is particularly ironic that altruism, in which women seem to specialize more than men (England and Farkas 1986, ch.3 and ch.4, England 1989), gets credited to men! (England 1993,p. 47)

Becker's failure to provide a theory of patriarchy is problematic here. Only a theory of patriarchy could help explain this issue. Becker's efforts at noting how minute gender differences at birth can lead to major differences through gender nurturing effects are useful, but still fail to identify why masculinity is affirmed over femininity.

Furthermore, Becker's analysis is ahistorical. Even if we agree that under capitalism access to market work determines power allocations (something that Becker also doesn't take note of), we then reach the incorrect conclusion that capitalism either creates patriarchy or exacerbates it.

In fact, anthropological studies have found that patriarchy is deeply embedded in virtually all societies. Patriarchy is really a broad name for gender-creating processes that favor men over women. However, the degree of female subordination is not constant.

Anthropologists agree that women's unique ability to produce children means that childrearing has been women's work. However, Joan Huber (1991) argues that, even though women still remain subordinate, how well childrearing relates to the kinds of labor valued in the society determines the relative power of women. Access to and control over the distribution of goods produced outside the family is key to the relative power of women. For example, hunters are more powerful than gathers. Because women could not hunt while pregnant or breast feeding (the latter lasting for up to four years after birth due to the absence of safe alternatives), women had relatively low positions in such societies. By contrast, in some agricultural societies, women fared better because their childrearing duties meshed better with working in food production. The critical distinction is access to public labor as opposed to being restricted to family domestic labor. To the extent that women are denied this full public stature, they are subordinated (Sacks 1974).

Functional sociology

It is important, therefore, to develop the relationship between economics and patriarchal gender-creating processes within capitalism. Functional sociology, while developing a theory based on complementary roles, has generally failed to adequately provide a tie between the two.

Functional sociology led by Talcott Parsons (1954) has located the masculine and feminine differences outside the economy. In this sense, Parsons and Becker share common footing. Parsons sees people acquiring status through achievements, possessions, authority, power and membership in kinship groups. Following the efficiency argument of the neoclassical economists, he argues that the occupational system in industrial society requires a high degree of social mobility. This mobility is essential so that the people who are most talented in particular areas are able to effectively move through social classes in order to find the occupation most suited to their talents. This way maximum productivity is achieved.

Parsons sees the occupational system coexisting with the values of the family. Equality of opportunity is not found within the family, creating a possible tension with the broader values of American society. However, Parsons believes the family acts as an adaptive cushion to minimize the strain between family life and the functional needs of industrial society.

The key aspects of this adaptation are the separation of sex roles within the family. This separation controls competition within family, enabling it to maintain important altruistic elements. Men fulfill instrumental roles, while women fulfill expressive roles. These functional roles yield a sexual division of labor where men specialize in market work and women specialize in household capital:

> It seems quite safe in general to say that the adult feminine role has not ceased to be anchored primarily in the internal affairs of the family, as wife, mother and manager of the household, while the role of the adult male is primarily anchored in the occupational world, in his job and through it by his status-giving and income-earning functions for the family. Even if, as seems possible, it should come about that the average married women had some kind of job, it seems unlikely that this relative balance would be upset; that either the roles would be reversed,

or their qualitative differentiation in these respects completely erased. (Parsons and Bales 1956,pp. 14-15 quoted in Beechery 1978,pp. 161-162)

Because the wife derives status from her husband, the two share the same status, maintaining stability. The persistence of the nuclear family results from social, psychological and biological factors. Socially, the family adapts to manage the transition between childhood and industrial society-based adult life. During this socialization, the family also psychologically fulfills the needs of the individual. Finally, the family is a useful reproductive unit as it corresponds with the fact that women bear and nurse children.

Yet as Veronica Beechery (1977) notes this analysis makes women's oppression primarily an issue of culture, rather than economics. By assigning women the same status as their husbands, female stratification, independent of capitalist production based classes, is underdeveloped. Thus, Parsons does not develop a model for integrating a study of capitalism and patriarchy.

Marx and Engels

By contrast Frederick Engels (1891) offers a materialistic theory of women's oppression. While his historical view of classless societies as being egalitarian is generally viewed as incorrect in light of more recent anthropological evidence (Hartmann 1974; Connell 1987), he does demonstrate a mechanism by which private property leads to, or reinforces, the subordination of women. Private property is not mere possessions, but ownership of income-producing resources. When a society becomes based on male-owned private property, men have particular interests in dominating women to regulate their reproductive abilities and to ensure heirs. Furthermore, women themselves become instruments of production for their husbands' benefit. Hence, women become restricted to the domestic sphere. This general historical argument is incomplete as not all men own private property and in some societies women can own and inherit property and still be subordinate (Sacks 1974), but as a representation of how in Europe private property reinforced patriarchy it is useful as it ties materialism to patriarchy.

However, in the context of capitalism, Karl Marx and Frederick Engels overemphasize economics and subsume patriarchy into capitalists class relations (Eisenstein 1979). In *The Economic and Philosophical Manuscripts* (1964) Marx compares women as chattel with the proletarian laborer under capitalism:

Finally, this movement of opposing universal private property finds expression in the animal form of opposing to *marriage* (certainly *a form of exclusive private property*) the *community of women* in which a woman becomes a piece of *communal* and *common* property ... Just as woman passes from marriage to general prostitution, so the entire world of wealth (that is, of man's subjective substance) passes from the relationship of exclusive marriage with the owner of private property to a state of universal prostitution with the community. (1964,p. 133)

In *The German Ideology* (1986) Marx and Engels argue that the role of the family and division of labor within it change under capitalism. The division of labor becomes inextricably tied to private property:

the *division of labour* implies the possibility, nay the fact that intellectual and material activity – enjoyment and labour, production and consumption – devolve on different individuals, and that the only possibility of their not coming into contradiction lies in the negation in its turn of the division of labor ... With the division of labour, in which all these contradictions are implicit, and which in its turn is based on the natural division of labour in the family and the separation of society into individual families opposed to each other, is given simultaneously the *distribution*, and indeed the *unequal* distribution, both quantitatively and qualitatively, of labour and its products, hence property: the nucleus, the first form, of which lies in the family, where wife and children are the slaves of the husband. This latent slavery in the family, though still very crude, is the first property... Division of labour and private property are, moreover, identical expressions: in the one the same thing is affirmed with reference to activity as is affirmed in the order with reference to the product of the activity. (1986, pp. 52-53)

The exploitation of women becomes tied to bourgeois institutions and ceases to have an independent identity. For Marx and Engels division of labor and private property are *identical*, as the family is destroyed as an institution by the forces of capitalism:

The bourgeois sees in his wife a mere instrument of production. On what foundations is the present family, the bourgeois family, based? On capital, on private gain ... The bourgeois claptrap about the family and education, about hallowed co-relation of parent and child, becomes all the more disgusting the more, by the action of modern industry, all family ties among the proletarians are torn asunder, and then children transformed into simple articles of commerce and instruments of labor. (1954 [1848],p. 50)

While Marx and Engels were responding to the excesses of the industrial revolution, the family, in fact, represents a semi-autonomous institution within capitalist social relations. This partial independence suggests that they underplayed the interaction between capitalism and patriarchy as displayed through households. Rather their focus was on capital and capitalist social relations which they thought would engulf familial social relations. Although capitalism does impinge on household social relations, the process needs much greater elaboration.

Marxist-Feminists

The 1970s saw the first attempts to apply Marxian analysis of household labor in what became known as the 'domestic-labor' debate. The question centered on whether the production of use-values by the housewife affected the value of labor power, where the value of labor power is the underlying determinant of the total wages paid.

Wally Seccombe (1974) argues that the housewife's labor is necessary labor, that she creates value. The value of the housewife's labor equals the cost of maintenance of the housewife. Since in Marxian analysis, the wage equals the labor cost of reproducing labor power, part of the wage reflects value created by the housewife. Purchased commodities are not in final consumption form and she adds her labor to these commodities in order to produce the labor power of the male wage earner. The wage equals sustenance for laborer and domestic laborer:

When the housewife acts directly upon wage-purchased goods and necessarily alters their form, her labour becomes part of the congealed mass of past labour embodied in labour power. The value she creates is realised as one part of the value of labour power achieves as a commodity when it is sold. All this is merely a consistent application of the labour theory to the reproduction of labour power itself, namely that all labour produces value when it produces any part of a commodity that achieves equivalence in the market place with other commodities. (1974,p. 9)

John Harrison (1973) also asserts that domestic labor produces value, but rather than seeing it embodied in the value of labor power, Harrison envisions it as being usurped by the capitalist in the form of greater surplus value, since the capitalist does not need to pay the worker as much. This argument has also been extended to suggest that the absence of a 'family wage' for husbands under capitalism leads to conditions where the wife must work and the resulting loss of domestic labor creates great misery for the working class, including a poor quality labor force and high infant mortality (Coulson, Mugas, and Wainwright 1975).

Jean Gardiner (1975) questions how one can measure the wife's value contribution. The fact that women are paid the value of their sustenance and their products are not valued suggests that there is no exploitation within the household (explained below). Nonetheless, she concludes that domestic labor helps depress the wages of wage earners.

The nonexploitation of domestic labor is a key theoretical point, most firmly established by Herbert Gintis and Samuel Bowles (1981). They distinguish between the value of labor power as the real wage and the cost of reproducing labor power (cost of living) as those commodities bought with the real wage *plus* the household labor added to those commodities. However, if we are to consider the homemaker's wage as coming out of the wage worker's wage, then it must be measured in the commodities which she consumes. The following equations develop the logic of their argument:

Defining variables:
- Worker's value of labor power = real wage
- Worker's cost of reproducing labor power = cost of living
- Commodities consumed by worker = C_w
- Commodities consumed by homemaker = C_h
- Labor of homemaker = L_h.

Implications of the definitions:
Note that the real wage = $C_w + C_h$
While the cost of living = $C_w + L_h$
If both are to be equal,
real wage = $C_w + C_h = C_w + L_h$ = worker's cost of living.
This implies $C_h = L_h$.

But what does $C_h = L_h$ represent? It represents the hours worked by the homemaker in exchange for a commodity bundle. If this is an equivalent exchange, then the commodity bundle should contain an equivalent quantity of labor.

The homemaker is not exploited in a Marxian sense! The wage worker sells (the use-value of) his labor power to the capitalist and receives a wage in exchange. Because the productive value of the use-value of labor power exceeds its exchange-value, the capitalist obtains surplus value, and, therefore exploits the worker. However, the wage of the homemaker is equal to the commodities she consumes, which in turn is equal to the productive use-value of her labor. There is no exploitation!

Besides demonstrating no exploitation, Gintis and Bowles reveal the capital-bias of the domestic labor debate. As Sylvia Walby also notes the key questions were not the relationship between husbands and wives, but between wives and capital:

> The debate about domestic labour thus occurs in a context that takes as a basic presumption the centrality of capital and is merely concerned with the exact delineation and relation of the elements of this system. This framework seriously limits the types of questions and answers which are possible in the issue of how to understand gender relations ... Most of these writings have very little analysis of gender inequality and are based on a mere presumption that capitalism is the problem rather than patriarchy or men. Thus the most important question is settled *a priori*. The interest that men, and in particular husbands, may have in the continuation and shaping of domestic work are almost totally neglected. (Walby 1986,p. 20)

Hence, the domestic labor debate does little to settle the relationship between patriarchy and capitalism. More recently an attempt to more effectively bridge Marxism and patriarchy has been attempted by Harriet Fraad, Stephen Resnick and Richard Wolff (1989). Rather than focus on the relationship between capital and domestic wives, they focus on the patriarchal relationship between a wage earning husband and domestic wife and analyze it as a class process.

They adopt the feudal mode of production as the best equivalent for this relationship, since feudalism represents an exchange of unequal use-values or the direct appropriation of labor time without compensation. Hence, they see the wife as performing surplus labor – labor beyond what is necessary to reproduce herself. By using this framework, they adopt a Marxian methodology to present surplus extraction within the home.

Their theory then centers on the allocation of work effort by the housewife, whether for herself or other family members, most notably the husband. They note two noneconomic factors intervening in the relationship so as to reproduce gender processes: ideology of love and gender ideology. The ideology of love works to disguise the labor of women within the home by turning it into a metaphor for expressing love. 'Through this ideology, the love of one human being for another becomes a means to facilitate class exploitation between them' (Fraad, Resnick and Wolff 1989,p. 25).

Gender ideology reinforces the gender division of labor, based on female passivity as being best fitted for the home and male aggression as being best fitted for the competitive capitalist labor market. This particular gender ideology is reinforced both through religious and cultural beliefs as well as a pressure on women to validate their mothers' lives by repeating the roles taught them by their mothers (Chodorow 1978).

Fraad, Resnick and Wolff more effectively link the concepts of capitalism and familial patriarchy by noting that a fall in the wage-earner's income may place additional stress on the housewife to increase her surplus labor to maintain the husband's living standard. They note the possible options of such wage-earners as:

- increasing the rate of exploitation of their wives;
- increasing the number of individuals who do surplus labor in the household, namely children or servants; and
- increasing the productivity of the household.

The first option represents a direct confrontation between the husband and wife. The second transfers this confrontation to others. The third means the husband gives up wage goods for himself in order to improve the productivity of his wife:

> To secure his feudal class position, ... the husband uses his cash wages not only to buy means of consumption, to reproduce the labor power he sells to the capitalists [,sic] he also transfers some of his wages to make the cash feudal subsumed class payments to reproduce his feudal household. (1989,p. 46)

Fraad et al. argue that this presents the possibility that payments to reproduce his household and reproduce his own labor power may exceed his cash wages. This inadequacy leads to either a loss of his own health, taking on a second job, or a redirection of goods from his wife's maintenance to his:

> Women are caught in a particular dilemma. To openly resist the demands of their men and their feudal position undermines their own un-

derstanding of their role in the household and in society at large ... Women's identities are at stake.

... the most common choice for women is to seek new income generating positions outside the household, while usually remaining in feudal bondage. They may supplement their husbands' wages with their own while still performing feudal surplus labor at home. (1989,p. 48)

The authors additionally note other reasons motivate women to sell their labor, as 'even in prosperous times women may seek such employment because of their preferences for capitalist over feudal exploitation' (1989,p. 48).

In this explanation for the rising labor force participation of married women, we see the fundamental weakness of this particular distributional model. Fraad et al. become so centered on the dynamics within the home that they fail to integrate it with the broader capitalist social structure. By so focusing on the conflict within the household, they ignore areas of common interest for the family with respect to the capitalist social structure. This lack of common concern is also seen in the failure to recognize that the husband's wage provides services to the housewife; so that an implicit exchange does take place. What ties these two factors together is that commodity consumption determines both what the housewife receives from her husband's labors and in part determines a relationship with the capitalist social structure.

Gender-creating processes and patriarchy

Gender-creating processes, while only briefly touched on by Fraad *et al.*, do provide a useful insight into patriarchy. Patriarchy, to be analytically useful, must be a dynamic concept. Too often it has remained fixed. Patriarchy must be considered as an historical concept, subject to change, rather than simply a descriptive term for sexism. Frequently patriarchy assumes only a descriptive function such as the following:

Patriarchy, for me, refers to a system of male householdship based on the domination, in the family household, of the father/husband over the mother/wife and resident children. It is founded upon three intimately coupled, material cornerstones: (a) effective possession of, entitlement to and ultimate disposal rights over family property, including income, on a daily and/or intergenerational basis;(b) supervision of the labour of other family members;(c) conjugal rights of sexual access to and possession of one's spouse in marriage and custodial rights over children. (Seccombe 1980,p. 63)

A descriptive patriarchy is no more useful than the biological determinism of Becker (Fine 1992). The question, then becomes one of integrating patriarchal gender-creating and capitalist social processes. In so doing, it is critical to develop a relationship between individuals and social structure while avoiding the difficulties of sex role theory. Sex roles are situation-specific identities such as 'mother' or 'student', not master identities (Hughes 1945):

> Ultimately, then role theory is not social theory at all. It comes right up to a problem where social theory logically begins, the relationship between personal agency and social structure; but evades it by dissolving structure into agency. (Connell 1987, p. 50)

As an alternative, Connell suggests an historical and practical concept of gender relations which constructs and reconstructs gender roles. He focuses on how gender is constructed and reconstructed in everyday life. In so doing he is critical of those features of patriarchy which, independent of biological factors, are unable to explain why men and women couldn't switch places in the gender hierarchy. We need to conceptualize gender formation as an ongoing social process that is both reproduced and/or reshaped during the context of everyday life (West and Zimmerman 1987; Ferree 1990).

Materialism and patriarchy – an entry point

When patriarchy and capitalism have been interwoven, the debate has generally been whether women's labor force participation rates were limited by patriarchal forces within families (Sen 1980) or whether patriarchal forces within labor markets have acted to prevent women from entering labor markets (Walby 1986). Similarly the 'Family Wage Debate' concerning economic labor reforms that benefitted male workers (especially in Britain in the late nineteenth century) has centered on whether there existed a coincidence of interests between husbands and wives to restrict market labor supply in order to push up market wages and provide adequate home use-values or between capitalist and proletarian men to preclude women from paid employment. Jane Humphries (1977) has argued for the former explanation for late nineteenth century Britain. In this case, the contest is between labor and capital.

By contrast Michele Barrett and Mary McIntosh (1980) and Sylvia Walby (1986) see it as contest between men and women. Barrett and McIntosh argue that the family wage has been detrimental to women. Walby sees male workers reacting to the monetary pressures on capitalists to hire cheaper female workers, which would threaten their patriarchal power. As commodity production outside capitalism disappeared for men, access to the capitalist labor market became critical for men to maintain their political advantage over women. Women's cheaper labor threatened their monetary dominance over them. Hence, she argues that male workers and male capitalists conspired to prevent women from gaining access to the labor market.

While the purpose here is not to take sides in this debate, one should note the timing of these struggles, the nineteenth century. The use-values associated with home production are clearly relevant to family sustenance during this time period. However, the family wage of 1890 would not be viewed as adequate in 1930, even adjusting for price increases. A shift had taken place that placed increased importance on market use-values. Many home-based items were now purchased on the market. Factory-made male clothing, which first appeared in standard sizes in the late nineteenth century (as a result of data gathered for Civil War uniforms), began to also become available for women (Strasser 1982). Canned foods became much more common, as today's well-known brand names: Heinz, Campbells, and Borden all appeared (Cowan 1983). Finally, frozen food was developed after Clarence Birdseye received a patent in 1925 for a new technique and by 1934, 39 million pounds were processed annually (Giedion 1948).

Thus, the issue of a family wage and of women's productive contribution to the family are interconnected with the role of consumption. Yet despite its critical importance, all participants in the debate abstract from this crucial issue.

Authors who have addressed the role of consumption with respect to women's labor market participation have either provided little theoretical rationale or simply demonstrated that the increased importance of market use-values has correlated with married women's labor market participation.

Marilyn Power (1983) suggests that married women stayed at home as long as their home work contributed significantly to the support of the family, but she does not analyze why particular use-values are valued more than others.

Following Thorstein Veblen, Clair Brown (1985, 1987) attempts to link an emulation theory of consumption to women's labor force participation. Although she provides a correlation between expenditure patterns and women's labor force participation, it is not integrated with patriarchy.

Brown's (1985) earlier work examines broad consumption patterns from 1918-1973. She argues that expenditures that are not complementary with or direct substitutes for a housewife's labor come to be valued less, leading women to work. Such a result is consistent with declining patriarchal use-values.

Brown suggests that all households will tend to emulate the spending patterns of higher social classes, regardless of whether the wife works. Hence, her model is based on the supposition that as incomes rise absolutely, lower income groups will emulate the expenditure pattern of higher social classes from an earlier era. Thus, a white wage earner group in 1960 would be expected to emulate the expenditure pattern of a 1950 white salaried income group with its additional or surplus income.

Using aggregate consumer expenditure survey data categorized into three social classes (laborer, waged, and salaried) for 1918, 1935, 1950, 1960 and 1973, Brown finds empirical support for her hypothesis. She finds that the percent of household-related expenditures defined as food, clothing and household operations expenditures decrease more than expected by her emulation model during the post World War II era. She interprets these changes in relative expenditures to suggest that use-values not associated with the home become increasingly important.

However, due to both the aggregate nature of her data as well as the broadness of the expenditure categories, these results are highly interpretive. Her household operations category, for instance, includes such items as cleaning products, household paper products, lawn and garden supplies, postage, appliance and furniture repair, gardening, babysitting, domestic services, and care of invalid, elderly and convalescents.

In her later work, Brown (1987) analyzes household expenditure patterns and nutritional composition of diets. From budgetary experts she deduces that most working class families did not achieve adequate nutrition until 1950. Thus, she argues that until adequate home nutrition was achieved households had an incentive to maintain a homemaking wife. While this argument ties a level of material development to a wife's allocation of her time, it is not integrated into the patriarchal social structure.

Brown suggests that the growth in 'female jobs' in the decades following World War II allowed these women to enter the work force. One still must question why wealthier women who presumably achieved adequate nutritional diets for their families at a much earlier date (and whose behavior would be emulated) had not already entered the work force. Clearly, the movement from homemaking to the work force is more complicated.

Conclusion

In summary we have reviewed Becker's efficiency view which sees the sexual division of labor as a rational outcome of households desiring to maximize the output from their collective resources. Any social valuation of masculine over feminine outputs is exogenous to this model. In this sense, Parsons, in emphasizing the adaptive and cultural roles of the family leading to a sexual division of labor, again divides the economic functions of family members from the social structure.

Conversely, while Marx and Engels see patriarchy as prior to capitalism, they believe that capitalism transforms patriarchy from making the wife the property of the husband to making her the property of the capitalist. Therefore, overthrowing bourgeois property relations will free women as much as it frees men. They err in the opposite direction by too strongly arguing for the relative importance of the economic over the cultural.

Marxist-Feminists in the 'domestic labor debate,' responding to the need to not conflate capitalism and patriarchy have ended up grafting the household to a capitalist-production centered analysis. On the other hand, Fraad, Resnick and Wolff overcompensate by using a Marxian methodology to analyze the household to the neglect of the broader social structure of capitalism.

Although the Marxist-Feminist works in the Family Wage debate and Fraad *et al* work to articulate patriarchy within the context of the social structure, they do not pay as much heed to materialism. Thus, a critical question develops as to how the patriarchal use-values relate to market use-values and how – and whether – conditions work within the social structure to change the relative importance of each. This critical question is the focus of this research. However, the nature of market use-values needs to be articulated within the context of the social structure of capitalism. This question is addressed in the next chapter.

Chapters four and five augment the work of Clair Brown by more carefully focusing on how the social structure of capitalism creates tensions for familial patriarchy by developing an ever growing social importance for use-values not manufactured within the home. Familial patriarchy, by restricting women to the home, depressed the households income earning potential. Yet as long as status differentials could be gained through homemaking, this trade-off was acceptable. However, homemaking as an ideal set by the wealthy is undermined by the process of market expansion and consumerism. Thus, the growth of women's labor force participation in the twentieth century emerges from a complex interaction of patriarchal gender-creating and capitalist class-creating processes.

Notes

1. While alternative neoclassical formulations based on intrahousehold bargaining have been developed, Becker's treatise remains dominant in part due to its ability to deliver results with less complication. Alternative theories have thus far remained highly abstract mathematical demonstrations of Nash bargaining outcomes and have not yet developed into a broader theory of family development (Manser and Brown 1980; McElroy and Horney 1981; Lundberg and Pollak 1993. For a nonmathematical summary see Lundberg and Pollak 1994). They argue that family members use either external threats like divorce or internal threats to bargain. However, to understand the exact formulation of how bargaining can affect results requires an a priori determination of *why* particular members prefer certain allocations (Schultz 1990). In an historical study, the *why* must be linked to the social structure, something not demonstrated in these models, but not necessarily beyond the use of this approach (Seiz 1991).

2. In fact, the woman could have an absolute advantage in both childrearing and market work and still by efficiency considerations remain within the home, if that's where she was comparatively more efficient.

3 Consumerism and the structure of capitalism

Why do we consume? Where do new needs or wants emanate from? If economics studies how people organize the production and distribution of goods and services designed to fulfill human needs, we are left with an intriguing question that goes beyond the scope of mainstream economic analysis, yet runs to the heart of economics. We recognize that we now live in a very materialistic world. Yet such tendencies were weaker only a few centuries ago. A transition occurred in the interim. Hence, the central issue in economic texts of scarcity – 'wants exceeding supply' – actually assumes that our current tendencies toward nonsatiated needs is both endemic and permanent. However, an examination of the historical record suggests that while the beginnings of consumer society may trace back to the sixteenth century (McKendrick 1982), we find substantial counterforces such as a Christian ethic which equated wealth acquisition and riches with sin (Viner 1991). The transformation increased substantially starting at the end of the nineteenth century and continuing through today.

This unending development of new needs or wants (NNOW) suggests that our theoretical understanding of why we behave as we do address these concerns. Hence, even though economics claims to be interested in how we go about satisfying human needs and wants, a satisfying answer can not take such needs and wants as given. In different social formations the nature and degree of these needs and wants are likely to change, which is just as much an economic question as the typical economic question of how people organize production and distribution to meet those needs and wants.

In this chapter I suggest a theoretical grounding of consumption behavior that underlies the rise in consumerism that largely coincided with the transition to a more bureaucratic, oligopolistic capitalism during the early twentieth century. Neoclassical economic theory, I argue, has ultimately turned economics into an offshoot of psychology. Individual motivation is assumed independent of the social structure. Relying instead on Marxian and institutional economic theory as well as sociology, I find more meaningful answers to the rise in consumerism. While I will suggest that consumerism has its origins in capitalist relations of production, that answer is too simplistic. Within the social structure of capitalism exist features that promote compensatory consumption – consumption designed to compensate for areas of human underdevelopment within the social structure. However, areas of human underdevelopment are not restricted to the site of paid production. Rather the site of paid production and the gender-based division of labor combine with intraclass mobility and class domination to form the basis of consumerism.

The limits of neoclassical consumer theory

Neoclassical theorists deserve credit for attempting to formulate a theory of consumption over a century ago. Consumption theory had not been adequately dealt with by classical economists, defined here as pre-Marxian and pre-Marginalist. However, in the process neoclassical consumer theory moved from class analysis to individual analysis. Despite their attempts to bring more rigor to consumption analysis, their lack of class analysis results in a theory which explains individual behavior but takes as given the social structure in which people reside.

Adam Smith, a classical economist, proclaimed: 'consumption is the sole end and purpose of production, and the interest of the producer ought to be attended to only so far as it may be necessary for promoting that of the consumer. This maxim is so perfectly self-evident that it would be absurd to attempt to prove it' (Elliott and Crownie 1975, p. 12). However, Smith's primary interest was not ascertaining the nature of the needs of the consumer but rather Smith concerned himself with production, growth and the distribution of product. The same held true for Ricardo and Marx. All three utilized a labor theory of value (i.e., wealth) creation in their analyses. The labor theory of value stressed that the market price was ultimately governed by the amount of labor embodied in the commodity. This supply-dominated theory of market price treated consumer demand, although a necessary precondition, as essentially secondary.

The ideological primacy of production was challenged by the marginalists' theory of value. W.S. Jevons stated as much concluding: 'the whole theory of Economy depends upon a correct theory of consumption' (Jevons 1871, p. 47). The same thought is echoed by Jevons' Austrian contemporary Karl

Menger: 'Economics must be founded upon a full and accurate investigation of the conditions of utility; and to understand this element we must necessarily examine the wants and desires of man' (1871, p. 39).

Marginalists turned the labor theory's primacy of supply in price determination on its head by stressing that until commodities were producible within the price range dictated by consumers, a sufficient market for them would not exist. Marginal analysis moved away from earlier utility theories of need that had relied on a universal theory of need. Classical economists, such as J.B. Say, using such a theory, could not explain why so called free goods like sunlight which were certainly needed had no price (Birken 1988). Marginalists by contrast argued that price equaled only the marginal benefit gained from the last unit purchased. Because marginal utility fell as one consumed more units of a product, consumers only purchased more quantity as long as the marginal benefit exceeded the price. Since the price equaled the marginal benefits on the last unit purchased, consumers necessarily paid less than the value of their total utility and thus gained from market exchange.

Marginalists had essentially provided a theoretical framework to support Adam Smith's contention that the consumer was sovereign in the capitalist marketplace. Yet taking such a step easily leads to post hoc reasoning. Philosopher Henry Walgrave Stuart (1907) correctly identified post hoc (or retrospective) reasoning as a key facet of our attempts to understand how we arrived at our present standard of living. By post hoc reasoning, humanity appears to evolve in a progressive fashion. Unsatisfied with their impoverished life, men fought for the freedom to pursue self-interest (capitalist markets) and then used that freedom to enhance their well-being. While this particular story is *possible*, the story is not only simplistic but deterministic, as it defines our current social formation as necessarily the pinnacle of human development.

This retrospective logic still underlies neoclassical economics. Results occur because people had preferences for these outcomes. Since consumers are sovereign within markets, markets necessarily produce what people desire. The inherent circularity (Broome 1991; Robinson 1962) in this type of argument is obvious. But even ignoring that criticism, neoclassical theory provides nothing in terms of a deeper social understanding for how consumer preferences, including the development of new needs or wants (NNOW), are formed. By assuming fixed preferences which are independent across consumers, the most important motivating features are exogenous to their analysis. Consumer choice exists independently of any analysis of the social structure of capitalism. As a result, they are unable to develop a theory of NNOW.

Sociologist Colin Campbell (1987) asserts that if utility theory were strictly followed, one would expect a tendency for stability as people held on to what was known, rather than give up a present want for a new one:

> While it could be argued that it is not irrational to believe others when they inform us that a new product will provide greater satisfaction than one currently consumed, this is to assume some standard for comparing satisfactions provided by different products as well as the idea that the tastes of individuals are equitable. Both of these assumptions are rejected by marginal utility theory. Equally, it could be suggested that it is not irrational for a consumer whose disposable income has grown to employ his surplus in trying a new product since he is not in this way losing any existing gratification. It is still the case, even here however, that a more rational strategy would be to use new wealth to consume more of what is already known as satisfying. This is indeed what traditional consumers typically do. (1987, p. 236)

This criticism is astonishing, because neoclassical economics is essentially the study of economic growth and how human needs are to be most efficiently met. Yet we know economic growth means the development of NNOW. Campbell's criticisms follow from two classic assumptions of the neoclassical model: ordinal utility functions and interpersonal independence of utility functions.

Neoclassical economics is more interested in consistent orderings of preferences than their actual content. Yet to obtain mathematically consistent orderings, certain rules must apply. Ordinal utility is required for transitivity, the axiom that if commodity bundle $A \succ$ (is preferred to) B and $B \succ C$, then $A \succ C$. Since utility is a metaphysical concept that cannot be measured, any particular measure used for mathematical convenience must be consistent for any positive monotonic transformation of it. Otherwise, the transitivity axiom of microeconomics can be violated. Let me provide a simple example.

Suppose we have three consumption bundles: A, B and C. $A \succ B$, $B \succ C$, and $A \succ C$. And suppose that we assign numbers to the utilities derived from those bundles:

$$U_a = 4$$
$$U_b = 3$$
$$U_c = 2.$$

We cannot assume from these numbers that A provides twice the satisfaction as C because the numbers are arbitrary. But because we can take any monotonic transformation of the utility function and preserve the order, we can maintain ordinal consistency. So if we make a monotonic transformation of the utility function by squaring it, we retain the same preference order: $A \succ B$, $B \succ C$, and $A \succ C$ as before:

$$U_a = 16$$
$$U_b = 9$$
$$U_c = 4.$$

All microeconomics can tell us is the preference ordering, not the degree of urgency of any particular preference. Furthermore, we cannot compare preferences across individuals. Thus, developing a theory of the origin of NNOW becomes difficult.

Instead, neoclassical theory suggests that NNOW are *latent* within each individual and revealed to us through actual purchases. Individuals are assumed to maximize their preference structures when they actually purchase items. Firms which produce goods that most clearly satisfy those preferences succeed; those firms which do not fail.

Many neoclassical economists defend the practice of presuming wants are fixed. By using that assumption as their starting point, they can then determine market price relationships. Says Milton Friedman:

> economic theory proceeds largely to take wants as fixed. This is primarily a cause of the division of labor. The economist has little to say about the formation of wants; this is the province of the psychologists. The economist's task is to trace the consequences of any given set of wants. The legitimacy of and justification for this abstraction must rest ultimately, in this case as with any other abstraction, on the light that is shed and the power of to predict that is yielded by the abstraction. (Friedman 1962, p. 13)

Hence, Lawrence Birken citing French anthropologist Louis Dumont argues 'the marginalist revolution made consumption – the satisfaction of idiosyncratic desire – the end of all human activity and thus immune from moral scrutiny' (Birken 1988, p. 31). Birken concludes: 'to evaluate value as subjective evaluation arising from the idiosyncratic and arbitrary taste was to root economic in the psychological... The economic could no longer be explained from within, but only from without by psychological laws' (Birken 1988, pp. 32, 35).

Reducing economics to psychology creates two problems. On the one hand, we lose the classical economists' original concern with social labor and social need. On the other, economic theory in its development risked losing its psychological foundations as psychology itself developed. In this work, I aim to focus on the former, but many have long argued that the latter has already occurred.

As institutionalist economist Hazel Kyrk noted seventy-five years ago, the narrow parameters of utility theory lack even a tenable psychological foundation. This shortcoming makes the theory indefensible as a theory of consumption, even though given tastes, it may provide a theory of price:

> It is fairly well established that [neoclassical economists] built their theory of human conduct, their so-called theory of consumption, upon a philosophy and psychology long since discredited and discarded ... We cannot recognize ourselves or our fellows in the hedonistic, individualistic calculators whom they described, nor find in their account any trace of the complexity of motives, impulses, and interests which lie behind market activities. This faulty and abstract explanation of choice, this unreal account of life and of the forces which are behind consumers' activities, may or may not affect the validity or their doctrine as a theory of exchange value or price, but it undoubtably does affect the adequacy of their theory of consumption. (1923, p. 17)

Numerous psychological studies verify Kyrk's objections, showing how the complexity of human behavior is actually not reducible to simple preference ordering and that axioms may be routinely violated (see for example Friedland and Robertson 1990). However, our real concern is not getting a particular individual's preferences right, but the nature of systematic social influence on preference formation.

Since neoclassical economists argue one cannot objectively measure utility across individuals, they have shied away from interpersonal utility comparisons. Still, they have generally not disagreed with the idea that preferences themselves are formed socially.

Mary McNally (1980) provides a way of conceptualizing how outside factors affect individual preferences. She suggests a dual utility determination model. A set of resources (raw materials, technology, etc.) and social processes generate a set of values. This value determination process is only partially under the individual's control. The individual then exercises those values in actual consumption choices. Figure 3.1 displays this simple schematic.

But how do neoclassical economists accommodate the notion that utility is partly socially determined? One attempt is to add ad hoc hypotheses into the utility function. Harvey Leibenstein (1950) demonstrated this option with the addition of *bandwagon*, *snob* and *Veblen* effects. These effects describe how

RESOURCES ➔ VALUES ➔(individual choice)➔ UTILITY
↗
SOCIAL PROCESSES

Figure 3.1 The utility formulation process

Source: McNally (1980, pp. 387-88).

people assign utility to consumption which enables them to join the crowd
(bandwagon), stand aloof from the crowd (snob), or to demonstrate their own
personal extravagance (Veblen). However, what this theory really implies is
that people's utility is formed and influenced by social forces. Why or how
these social forces come into play remains unknown. Leibenstein simply
wishes to demonstrate the ramifications for any particular good for which
bandwagon, snob or Veblen appeal would be a factor in addition to its independent utility in determining demand. More recent work has tried to formal-
ize interpersonal and intrapersonal effects (habits) in mathematical models,
but still fails to investigate the relationship between social structure and
NNOW (e.g., Pollack 1970). These models are partially helpful in that if we
can pinpoint social aspects of demand and add them to neoclassical models,
the models provide a deeper understanding of price determination.

In order to develop more coherent predictive models, neoclassical economists must assert a fixed motivational structure in detail (e.g., Lancaster 1971;
Stigler and Becker 1977). Rational choice theory suggests that an action be
utility maximizing, but does not mandate how you go about maximizing.
Hence, economists dictate the structure of utility functions, content and the
precise form when making predictions (Brennan 1990). In essence, the motivational behavior of agents is assumed. Yet this motivational behavior is precisely what must be discovered if the origin of NNOW is to be understood.
Lawrence Boland (1992) makes an even more telling criticism; the neoclassical results are arbitrary. Boland asks how do people know the shapes of their
indifference curves? If we really learn such things by doing, then it is entirely
possible that people with the same preference structure, income and prices
will choose *different* commodity bundles. Each may be attempting to maximize utility but may or may not be successful in doing so. As such and with
limited information, we can expect that people will take cues from their social
environment to aid them in this task.

When we introduce a broader social schemata which includes the class
structure of capitalism then it becomes possible to think that people's criteria

may be systematically biased or skewed in their process of determining the appropriate commodity bundle.

Social structure and the development of consumerism

The issue of consumerism's ascendancy is primarily linked to three features of the social structure: the structure of labor markets, the nature of class relations, and the impact of capitalist production on the gender division of labor within the home. First, the elimination of the labor-leisure option for male workers is both critical to the rise of mass consumerism as well as understanding how patriarchy interacts with consumerism, which I address in the next chapter. Second, the change in the structure of class relations, resulting from the ascendancy of a capitalist class which accompanies monopoly capitalism, helps to undermine the religious structure of society (with individual secularism replacing religious piety) and likewise removes social sanction to interclass mobility leading to upheavals at the top of the class hierarchy which filter down to the working class.

A more specialized division of labor

Urbanization has preceded but also correlated with the development of capitalism. Some aspects of consumerism have been tied to urbanization. Emile Durkheim's *Division of Labour in Society* (1984 [1893]) argues that population pressures on survival are the primary forces leading to the efficiency imperative of economics:

> If labour becomes increasingly divided as societies become more voluminous and concentrated, it is not because the external circumstances are more varied, it is because the struggle for existence becomes more strenuous.
>
> Darwin very aptly remarked that two organisms vie with each other more keenly the more alike they are. Having the same needs and pursuing the same purposes, they are everywhere to be found in rivalry. So long as they possess more resources than each needs, they can be still live cheek by jowl. But if each happens to increase in such proportions that appetites can no longer be sufficiently assuaged, war breaks out and it is the more violent the more striking the shortfall, that is, the numbers vying with one another are greater. (1984 [1893], pp. 208-09)

However, happiness is a complex calculus of pleasure and pain, where pain is weighted more heavily than an equal amount of pleasure. Durkheim notes that a division of labor with greater interdependence increases pain. People's existence becomes more tied up with the particular craft they practice, and if that craft comes into competition with a similar one as the economy becomes more advanced, one may lose one's livelihood and become an employee or foreman rather than a small employer or shopkeeper. As a result, division of labor in society also leads to higher levels of (egoistic) suicide and mental illness as people have difficulty adapting to the greater strains of a more complex society.

The cure for the pain according to Durkheim is consumption. Societies with a growing division of labor require economic growth and NNOW:

> Every new specialization has a result an increase and improvement in production. If this advantage is not the reason for the existence of the division of labour, it is a necessary consequence. As a result, lasting progress cannot be established unless individuals really feel the need for more abundant or better-quality products ... Yet from where may such demands spring?
>
> They are an effect of the same cause that determine the progress of the division of labour. Indeed we have just seen that progress is due to the greater fierceness of struggle. Now a more violent struggle does not occur without a greater deployment of forces, and consequently not without greater fatigue. Yet in order for life to continue the reward must always be proportionate to the effort; this is why nourishment that until then was sufficient to restore the organic equilibrium is henceforth insufficient. (1984 [1893], p. 214)

Thus consumption plays an important stabilizing influence for Durkheim by providing ever higher levels of pleasure to counterbalance the psychic pain which also grows in the society. These consumption needs, however, are not innate but of a social character. For Durkheim, material consumption must be seen as a functional part of social totality, not simply as evidence of progress:

> We see how different our view of the division of labour appears from the economists. For them it consists essentially in producing more. For us this greater productivity is merely a necessary consequence, a side-effect of the phenomenon. If we specialise it is not so as to produce more, but to enable us to live in the new conditions of existence created for us. (1984 [1893], p. 217)

Durkheim presents a clear integration of consumption and the origination of NNOW and social structure. Within his theory there is a dynamic interplay between the forces of production and consumer demand. However, his articulation of how consumption pleasure works to transcend the pressures of a society based on the division of labor is ultimately driven by population pressures, which provides only a crude basis for understanding social relations.

As an analysis, Durkheim's integration only provides a plausible starting point. However, regardless of the origin of specialization, it seems reasonable to see consumption development as a necessary corollary of great increases in production. Increased production necessitates increased consumption. Yet, the social meaning of consumption still needs refining. This social meaning follows from two particular avenues: a further development of the labor market and a cultural and class understanding of consumption norms.

The problem of labor-leisure choice

Social structure is an important element in Marxian analysis. In fact, most Marxists define capitalism by the presence of a class of wage laborers who must sell their labor in order to survive. Yet understanding survival requires a concept of need. Without removing wage labor from the area of voluntary exchange, capitalism cannot develop a consumer base as can be seen from neoclassical labor markets in historical perspective.

In conventional economic analysis, an increase in the wage leads to two opposing effects. On the one hand, a higher income results from the higher wage, which means that more goods are demanded. If we assume that leisure is a normal good, i.e., that demand for leisure increases with income, then a higher income enables the worker to buy more leisure by working less. Hence, the income effect is negative, meaning that an increase (decrease) in income leads to less (more) work being performed. On the other hand, leisure is not like other goods, because it is a direct substitute for wage-labor. Hence, to buy leisure by working less means to forgo income. Unlike other goods, the price of leisure is an implicit price, since its price is the foregone wage income. As the wage increases this 'price' of leisure increases, meaning one would demand less. Hence, the substitution effect is positive, as the wage increases (decreases), the worker substitutes wage labor (leisure) for leisure (wage labor).

The net result of these two effects is not clear. Instead economists work around this dilemma by postulating a backward bending labor supply curve. Until a worker reaches some wage threshold, her positive substitution effect outweighs her negative income effect, leading to increasing hours of labor market activity. Beyond the threshold, the negative income effect outpaces the positive substitution effect, creating a backward bend.

The labor supply curve exists within a social setting which conditions wage labor. These conditions include the choice to opt out from capitalist enterprise. Historically, when this scenario is the case, the capitalist has had great difficulty recruiting and maintaining a work force:

> It is a fact well known (wrote a mid[18th]-century commentator) ... that scarcity, to a certain degree, promoted industry and that the manufacturer (worker) who can subsist on three days work will be idle and drunken the remainder of the week ... The poor in the manufacturing countries will never work any more time in general than is necessary just to live and support their weekly debauches ... We can fairly aver that a reduction in wages in the woolen manufacture would be a national blessing and advantage, and no real injury to the poor. By this means we might keep our trade, uphold our rents, and reform the people in the bargain. (J. Smith, *Memoirs of Wool* (1747) quoted in Thompson 1963, p. 277)

Not only did the labor supply curve exhibit a backward bend, but it did so at a relatively low wage. Thus, this commentator postulated that a further reduction in the wage would elicit a greater amount of labor. The fundamental problem was that workers could make their own labor-leisure trade off choices. This being the case, they chose more leisure. As Stephen Marglin notes, 'As British internal commerce and its export trade expanded, wages rose and workers insisted in taking out a portion of their gains in the form of greater leisure' (1974, p.50).   The same phenomenon has been noted by anthropologist Marshall Sahlins in his studies of the impact of the integration of South American native cultures into market capitalism:

> Recruited as plantation hands, they frequently showed themselves unwilling to work steadily. Induced to raise a cash crop, they would not react 'appropriately' to market changes: as they were interested mainly in acquiring specific items of consumption, they produced that much less when crop prices rose, and that much more when prices fell off. And the introduction of new tools or plants that increased the productivity of indigenous labor might only then shorten the period of necessary work, the gains absorbed rather by an expansion of rest than of output. All these and similar responses express an enduring quality of traditional domestic

production, that it is production for use values, definite in its aim. (1972, p.86)

Control of the labor force is the primary problem facing these nascent capitalists. The remedy to this problem requires elimination of the labor-leisure option, so that the capitalist – and not the worker – dictates hours. As workers lost the choice to strictly control the hours of work, their choice came to be between not working – which they could not afford to do – and working full-time.

Establishing the lowest wage which elicited full-time labor supply required the elimination of other sources of sustenance for workers. The backward bend then no longer causes difficulty for capitalists as the process of forcing workers to devote their energies full-time to wage labor also creates the excess supply conditions to keep wages below the backward bend. Hence, the modern context is first of all premised upon the notion of capitalist control over workers.

Concomitant with this development was the increasing preference for goods over leisure. As workers lost the power to choose leisure, they developed a preference for goods. However, by what social process did this occur?

While workers resisted long hours, it does not seem to follow directly that would necessarily lead to a preference for goods. Rather the preference for goods develops because it meets both the needs of workers as well as the capitalists. Roy Rosenzweig (1983) describes how capitalists had to bribe Irish immigrant labor in Worcester, Massachusetts in the early nineteenth century to work by allowing alcoholic beverages on the job. Two reasons stand out for why this was necessary. First, as the workers labored eleven or more hours a day, they had little time for leisure outside their jobs. Thus, employers in order to maintain their workforce were required to provide some kind of substitute for that lost leisure time in the form of whiskey. However, implied in this response is the limited monetary needs of Irish immigrants. Because their communities were quite cohesive and a broader mass consumer culture had still not developed, they could achieve satiated wants. Nonetheless, they were proletarianized as wage income was essential for their survival. Thus, whiskey was an early solution to this labor-leisure choice problem. However, whiskey was an ineffective solution since it both lowered labor productivity and led to social crusades against excessive drinking.

Rosenzweig suggests that a social contract whereby drinking was eliminated from the workplace in the mid-nineteenth century corresponded with shorter hours. This change was not simply an issue only for Irish immigrants in Worcester. A New York carriage maker described the change before a US

Senate committee in 1883 on relationships between labor and capital: 'I can remember twenty or twenty-five years ago when our trade, even in our shop, there was a constant sending out for beer and spirits and it was universally permitted'. Now he noted such behavior, 'is a violation of rule which affords reason for discharge' (1983, p. 38).

However with somewhat greater leisure saloons instead became the workers' center of drinking, disorderly behavior, as well as subtle forms of class resistance. Temperance campaigns aimed to close the saloons in large part because this lifestyle was deemed inconsistent with the more reserved conservative culture of the ruling classes (Rosenzweig 1983).

Compared to saloon drinking, consumerism tends to be more consistent with the interests of the ruling classes. Because of this coincidence, Marxists often consider consumerism a form of 'false consciousness'. However, this position really reflects an underdevelopment of the link between social structure and consumption.

Part of this shortcoming results from the productive bias in Marx's work. Marx's focus on how capitalist relations of production created alienation and struggle did not carry over to his analysis of consumption, even though Marx noted the 'historical and moral element' which determined consumption (Wells 1992).

Throughout *Capital*, Marx assumed a fixed consumption basket at subsistence and that the value of labor power reflects the current value of that basket. Lebowitz (1982, 1991) has pointed out that Marx planned to drop this assumption in a future book on wage-labor, which he never got around to writing.

Like Durkheim, Marx suggests that alienation may contribute to consumption. However, Marx introduces class which Durkheim fails to do. Four kinds of alienated labor characterize the capitalist mode of production according to Marx: alienation from the product, from the production process, from him or her self and from capital (Elliott 1981). The worker is alienated from the product, for she produces something that she does not possess. Second, this work is forced and determined by the employer, creating alienation from the work process itself. Third, as work is deskilled and/or dictated from above, it fails to utilize the creative powers of humanity. The worker is alienated from humanity and therefore herself. Finally, since the worker labors for another and does not possess the product of her labor or control the work process, the worker is necessarily alienated from capital.

These forms of alienation were most explicitly presented in the *Economic and Philosophical Manuscripts of 1844* and they provide the philosophical foundation for his later work analyzing the capitalist mode of production.

However, the 1844 Manuscripts also mention alienated needs, as capitalists attempt to create new needs and place workers in a position of continual dependency (Elliott 1981). Yet the process by which alienated needs develop was not examined.

Marx's concept of commodity fetishism does provide an entry point into the social construction of individuals (Amariglio and Callari 1989). Commodities have a use-value, but that use-value is a social construction, which although tied to its exchange-value, is severed from the actual social relations of its production. People buy commodities because of what the commodity can do or culturally represents, but they rarely consider the workers who produced it when they make purchases. Hence, the commodity is both alive with cultural meaning and a lifeless form with no labor power seen as being embodied within it (Marx 1967 [1867]; Rose 1978; Taussig 1980). This live cultural meaning captures the freedom of individuals to constitute themselves by surrounding themselves with commodities or refurbishing old commodities into new cultural meanings with their labor. Thus, in contrast to the routine of the work place or home chores, commodities exhibit the ultimate 'freedom' of self-expression and social mobility (Willis 1970).

Moving from a use-value oriented society to a market society, changes the qualitative nature of consumption. Because the market sets monetary values upon commodities, it allows buyers to examine commodities independently of their use-value. While the market provides a means of valuation by which preferences may be realized, it does so by valuing things in terms of wealth. Yet money more than facilitates exchange. Money itself becomes valued and the utility which one gets from a commodity is not simply related to the commodity's use-value but to its present and future value on the market (Levine 1989).

These acts of exchange-value oriented consumption further reinforce labor market discipline on workers. As a worker, the worker-consumer seeks better pay, shorter hours and meaningful labor. As a consumer she seeks the best buy for the dollar. Since consumers buy many items produced by other workers, their purchase decisions affect the working conditions for other workers, not themselves. Thus, consumers have no direct incentive to take issues other than price or quality into account when making purchases and as a result will tend to undermine high quality work place standards. In order to maximize their consumption bundle, consumers necessarily support those capitalist firms which produce at the lowest cost. Given the importance of capitalist control, this act of maximization will reinforce the most effective exploitative kinds of capitalist control. The worker-consumer reinforces her own worker status and undermines her ability to obtain better working conditions. Thus, we can state that a capitalist market society displays consumer sovereignty because the desires of the consumer are prioritized over those of the worker (Lane 1991).

Each worker-consumer then stands in perpetual struggle with herself. By placing these constraints on themselves, worker-consumers effectively make it much more difficult to obtain greater leisure, meaning that greater consumption becomes the direction of social reproduction, not greater leisure.

Consumption as a method of 'free' personal expression

Social emulation The process by which consumption tastes disperse within society was first suggested by Thorstein Veblen (1953 [1899]). Veblen integrates issues of social class with those arising from a society with a division of labor. The chief motivating factor for Veblen is status.

As industrial activity replaces predatory activity in the society, the signs of status change. When hunting is the most prized activity, the symbols of successful hunts, animal heads, are revered as signifying status. As the society becomes more industrial, proceeds from the control of property have this significance:

> And it is even more to the point that property now becomes the most easily recognized evidence of a reputable degree of success as distinguished from heroic or signal achievement. It therefore becomes the conventional basis of esteem. Its possession in some amount becomes necessary in order to have any reputable standing in the community. It becomes indispensable to accumulate, to acquire property, in order to retain one's good name. When accumulated goods have in this way once become the accepted badge of efficiency, the possessions of wealth presently assumes the character of an independent and definitive basis of esteem. (Veblen 1953 [1899], p. 37)

The nature of conspicuous consumption in part depends on urbanization. Veblen notes how consumption standards are less in rural communities where social ties are stronger than urban areas where the ties are greater but more superficial. These same issues are extended by historians to population movements in general which coincide with a move toward material goods commencing in seventeenth century Western Europe and the United States:

> In a world in motion, migrants and travelers needed a standardized system of social communications. They required a set of conventions they

61

could carry with them that signified anywhere they went the status they enjoyed at home. So ordinary people adopted and then adapted to their own various special needs a system of courtly behavior borrowed ultimately from a protocol developed in France and disseminated though Amsterdam and London to provincial England and the colonies. Standardized architectural spaces equipped with fashionable furnishings became universally recognized settings for social performances that were governed by internationally accepted rules of etiquette. (Carson 1994, pp.523-524)

The process of migration is especially striking for the American colonies with immigrants from different locales within Britain and later from different countries, settling and forming new communities. An intriguing example of this desire of consumption conformity is suggested by Ronald Hoffman (1994) when he describes the elaborate preparations of Samuel Adams for the First Continental Congress in Philadelphia. Adams had only left Boston once before to attend Harvard. Adams' friends were so concerned with how his dress might be perceived that he was outfitted with a new wardrobe and wig. Yet upon arrival, delegates found further dissimilarities despite their supposedly common social class. Social convention had not quite caught up to appearances.

But in the context of urbanization, appearances may be sufficient. Veblen sees coinciding with urbanization, the decline of formal class distinctions and their replacement with income (consumption)-based ones. People work toward self-improvement by seeking to emulate the consumption norms of the next highest strata.

Veblen does not limit conspicuous consumption to public display. As the conspicuous culture develops, it comes to define norms even for personal consumption which others may never see. Hence, undergarments and some household appliances also fall prey to conspicuous desires which have been so completely ingrained within the individual that the entire preference set is effected.

Veblen's emulative model, however, runs counter to some methods of social distinction and fails to distinguish why leisure failed to also become emulative. Veblen suggests social competition or the desire to improve one's social standing in urban market societies is the driving force behind emulation. This implies that comparison with peers leads to dissatisfaction and renewed efforts to improve status. 'Studies in reference group theory have shown, however, that this is by no means the necessary outcome of comparisons made with those whom we consider to be our equals, and that satisfaction with one's position is just as likely an outcome as dissatisfaction' (Campbell 1987, p.51).

Bridge goods However, Campbell's criticism, based on the work of Merton (1968), only demonstrates that people must seek satisfaction from certain accomplishments, especially when other areas create disconcert. People adopt consumption trajectories where particular consumption goods become bridges to an alternative and better future. Through these consumption-good-bridges to an alternative reality, the consumer can escape her present situation. These goods tend to be beyond one's immediate means, but still enable one to set a consumption trajectory in order to at some point claim these items. The consumption item then becomes the means to achieving that better life. However, once the item becomes realized, the ideal is then temporarily merged with reality, but as the romanticized good cannot compete with its actual use-value, the owner then forms a new bridge to an alternative more lofty item (McCracken 1988).

Grant McCracken links these bridge goods with the 'Diderot effect'. Diderot (1713-1794) wrote how a friend's gift disturbed his consumption patterns in 'Regrets on Parting With My Old Dressing Gown':

> This essay begins with Diderot sitting in his study bemused and melancholic. Somehow his study has undergone a transformation. It was once crowded, humble, chaotic, and happy. It is now elegant, organized, beautifully appointed, and a little grim. Diderot suspects the cause of the transformation is his new dressing gown.
>
> This transformation, Diderot tells us, took place gradually and by stages. First, the dressing gown arrived, a gift from a friend. Delighted with his new possession, Diderot allowed it to displace his, 'ragged, humble, comfortable old wrapper.'
>
> This proves the first step in a complicated and ultimately distressing process. A week or two after the arrival of the dressing gown, Diderot began to think that his desk was not quite up to standard and replaced it. Then the tapestry on the study seemed a little threadbare, and a new one had to be found. Gradually, the entire study, including its chairs, engravings, bookshelf and clock were judged, found wanting, and replaced.
>
> All of this, Diderot concludes, is the work of an 'imperious scarlet robe [which] forced everything else to conform to its elegant tone' (1964, p. 311). Diderot looks back with fondness and regret to his old dressing gown, and its 'perfect accord with the rest of the poor bric-a-brac that filled my room ... Now the harmony is destroyed. Now there is

no more consistency, no more unity, and no more beauty' (1964, p.311). This unhappy revelation constitutes what is likely the first formal recognition of a cultural phenomenon here called the 'Diderot unity' and the 'Diderot effect.' (1988, p. 118-119)

Thus, contrary to neoclassical utility theory, which suggests that goods have utility in and of themselves, this effect implies that their worth may be complementary with other goods and likewise erode the utility of goods which are perceived inferior. Since people surround themselves with consumption goods – they behave protectively – but bridge items threaten this continuity, leading to upward ratcheting consumption via the Diderot effect.

Self-creation This notion of life plans interacting with commodities reflects a self-centeredness which was not present in earlier European culture. Historically, Campbell (1987) finds that the orientation toward self-centeredness is a relatively new orientation. In pre-capitalist cultures emotions are seen as inherent aspects of reality which exert their influence over humans. In the Middle Ages 'fear' and 'merry' referred to attributes of external events – the former an unexpected happening and the latter as characteristic of a day or occasion. 'Awe' was ascribed to God rather than man's reaction to God's presence (Barfield 1954).

Under capitalism, the source of emotions has shifted from an environmental source of emotions where the person is the neutral receiver to the reverse where emotions emanate from the person. Max Weber (1965) referred to this disappearance of 'spirits' which operated in nature as 'disenchantment'.

The growth of self-consciousness is revealed in the spread of 'self' prefix words which first appeared in the English language in 16th and 17th centuries and were widely adopted by the eighteenth century (Barfield 1954). It is also represented in the change of religion from an external entity to a self-generated choice for individuals (Berger, Berger and Kellner 1974).

This change in orientation also affected the interpretation of dreams. Pre-capitalist dreaming has an external agency component, leading them to be interpreted as visions:

> In modern, self-illusory hedonism, the individual is much more of an artist of the imagination, someone who takes images from memory or the existing environment, and rearranges or otherwise improves them in his mind in such a way that they become distinctly pleasing... Not only does modern man take pleasures in his day-dreams, but obtaining en-

joyment from them radically changes his view of the place of pleasure in real life. (Campbell 1987, p. 78)

Dreams become a motivating force to cause individuals to withdraw from engagement with real life in order to escape into fantasy for enjoyment. Campbell builds upon this aspect of dreaming in the context of a self-oriented ideology to suggest that people utilize consumer goods and services as objects of imaginative interaction. However, Campbell stresses that imagination is always more pleasing than reality, so that once a purchase has been made and the use-value moves from the non-tangible world to the tangible world, the user is ultimately disappointed. Then the cycle begins anew to remove the psychic pain.

In contrast to Durkheim, for Campbell the psychic pain is not related to the strain created by the division of labor, rather it is entirely built upon the self-centered freedom to construct an alternative reality. As dreaming has limits due to the nature of pleasure gained from these dreams, the physical product is necessary to bring the dream to reality. Yet once the products disappoint, people again retreat into their dream world to create new realities. Campbell considers his model's strength that it is entirely self-generated. Imitation and emulation are not necessary to drive this system.

Yet such reductionism makes the social structure of society unnecessary in his theory as well. Certainly the original changes that led to greater self-centeredness had a basis in the interaction between individuals and the existing social structure. So to suggest that social structure is not necessary for understanding NNOW is also an example of intellectual fantasy on the part of Campbell.

The construction of social consciousness, with an integral focus on self, is a theme of Peter Berger, Brigitte Berger and Hansfield Kellner's *The Homeless Mind* (1974), which specifically relates consciousness to social structure. Berger *et al.* tie economic development to a corresponding socio-cultural process which impacts each individual's understanding of self. In particular, they attribute the psychic pain of Durkheim to internalized fragments within the self. Those engaging in wage labor at an institution outside the home must adopt both a work-self and a home-self – each with a separate consciousness and mode of behavior. The work place requires the wage earner to visualize his or her co-workers as concrete individuals who are simultaneously anonymous functionaries doing tasks within the firm. Likewise, the wage earner must be able to see him or her self as being both an individual and an anonymous functionary. The ability to visualize this fragmentation is critical for succeeding within the work place. Individuals must be able to relate to co-workers, while simultaneously recognizing that each job within the organization exists independently of the particular person filling it.

Because wage earners must manage their emotions at work, they are limited in their ability to use work as a means of self-expression. The home then becomes the center for their individuality. As the home is perceived as a center of consumption rather than production, individuals interact with commodities to build that self which is denied at the work place.

Berger *et al.* also point to the difficulties found in a formally classless society. Each individual, rather than inheriting a family occupation or class role, is left with the freedom to determine his or her own path. However, as teenagers become young adults, they must select from this multitude of career paths to determine their life's plan. Within this context, they continually write and rewrite their life biography, but each successive rewrite must deal with the frustration of not living up to their prior expectations. Consumption goods become an important marker for an alternative definition of success.

A social consensus on luxuries Yet what determines which particular consumption goods will be sought? Under capitalism formal class distinctions give way. Whereas sumptuary laws were imposed to preserve class distinctions in dress under feudalism (Kyrk 1923), in capitalism no such barriers exist – except financial limits.

Veblen's analysis was aimed primarily at the nouveau riche of his time. He spent considerable time, noting how their acts of conspicuous consumption and conspicuous leisure demonstrated to others that they did not engage in manual labor and had plenty of money. Yet, this demand for leisure did not trickle down with the same intensity as the demand to consume. Veblen's efforts do not provide sufficient grounds for understanding this discrepancy. Earlier I provided that the reason for this failure is that for workers the labor-leisure choice is removed.

We must further ask why imitation – rather than innovation – is used for social differentiation, especially when new items of conspicuous consumption might originally be innovative (Campbell 1987).

Hazel Kyrk's *Theory of Consumption* (1923) further develops the ideas of Veblen. Kyrk presents a sociological explanation for imitation over innovation. She suggests that new consumption expenditures will generally occur only when one has surplus income. However, those with large amounts of income are likely to first reach a point where they have more income than they have immediate plans for – they exceeded their bridge ambitions. When they seek to use this money, there are a number of limits on its use. First, to innovate might also mean being eccentric, a risk not everyone is willing to take. Second, experimentation requires thought, constructive ability, and the time to carry out one's plans. In other words, experimentation requires leisure. Because leisure is socially restricted, choice leads to imitation. With additional income, people generally upgrade their current consumption, such as buying better transportation, rather than buying a greater quantity of transportation. In addition, cost considerations mean those items which are mass produced, rather than customized, will be chosen by the working class. Thus, the general direction of innovation is largely determined by those with leisure. As a result, Kyrk notes that, as a society, we have a remarkable consensus over what constitutes luxuries:

> How is it that we know with such certainty as we do know, just what the luxuries of life are, those nonessential, but highly desirable, articles which are now out of reach? We know because *we accept* as such the goods and activities of the elite or the superior social classes. (1923, p. 260 emphasis added)

Campbell (1992) questions whether the wealthy are, in fact, the source of innovation. Not all consumption styles flow from the rich. Paul Romberg for instance observed in the 1970s:

> many standards in fashion have been set, not so much by the upper or even middle classes, as by the declasse anti-class youth, and counterculture. Long hair, head bands, beads, ... and all the other paraphernalia of the counterculture costume, not only mock the materialist status symbols of the established classes, but have successfully spread into the enemy camp ... When blue denim work shirts are selling at New York's Bloomingdales and when rock-star Mick Jagger is voted one of the world's best-dressed men, there is obviously something wrong with the theory that sees fashion styles established at the top and trickling down. (1974, pp. 493-494)

Other examples are easily found. In the early 1990s Los Angeles teenagers partially bared their boxers by wearing beltless over-sized pants, a practice initiated by Latino-American male teenagers in Southern California to emulate ill-fitting prison garb (Vigil 1988) and soon spread across the country (Mitchell 1992).

These critiques are centered on the myriad of ways in which goods enable us to communicate with each and establish an identity (Douglas and Isherwood 1980; Leiss 1983). The fact that fashionable styles may come from the clothing innovations of social groups that appear to have relatively little money to spend on clothing is perhaps not surprising. In 1991 despite average incomes 1/3 less than whites, African-Americans spent slightly more per capita on clothing than whites. Many African-American urban youths find wearing designer fashions important in establishing their identity. It becomes a method by which they stand out and feel good about themselves in an otherwise depressing environment (Seo 1993). Their styles are not necessarily copied for their inherent good looks, but because for varying social reasons, young people seek to identify with a perceived element of these groups – whether it be alternative lifestyles with the counterculture or the perceived strength and independence of street gangs.

However, our focus here is misplaced because we are dealing with a marginal consumption group, teenagers and young adults, who in time generally do adopt more orthodox patterns of behavior. More stable and emulative behavior occurs with respect to furnishings and real estate, which represent a more fixed social identity. Hence, the wealthy due to their relative abundance of financial resources and the social esteem in which they are held have their consumption socially validated. As a result, we should not dismiss Kyrk's observation on the general consensus we have as a society on what constitutes our consumption luxury desires.

Class mobility, consumerism and positional struggle

As we examine this theory of the development of consumerism, we see a number of critical factors. Workers who historically had fixed needs have the nature of their needs change as society becomes less class structured and more transient. Greater class mobility which is characteristic of capitalism, even though it is largely nominal in practice, validates people's desire to emulate those in higher classes.

Campbell (1993) has questioned whether imitation reflects a desire for social status or that one is merely impressed by the physical attributes of the commodity. Duesenberry's (1948) demonstration effect would be akin to this second form of motivation as opposed to Goffman's (1959) ideas that one is always motivated by how one presents oneself to others. Regardless of the actual motivation, one still cannot divorce physical attributes from the social environment in which they are placed. People desire a Ferrari, not just because it is a fast car, but because it is a very rare and expensive car. People who own 'superior' commodities turn heads. However, the difference between an eccentric's invention and a socially legitimate display should also not be discounted. Hence, Campbell is correct to state: 'it is more realistic to see conduct as directed at reassuring oneself of one's moral worth and although this is sometimes achieved by first impressing others, a crucially different motivational structure is involved' (1993, p. 46).

Unlike the style of dress of teenagers which may be easily imitated, much consumption is oriented toward acquiring 'positional goods' in order to develop 'cultural capital' (Hirsch 1977; Bourdieu 1984). As the concept of class was muted by consumerism, the horizontal interdependence of status cultures within class structures was threatened:

> The elements of the status cultures include styles of dress, forms of food preparation, or aesthetic preferences that the groups have succeeded in monopolizing, through sumptuary laws, control of ancillaries to consumption (e.g. concert halls or cooking classes), or choices of elements that others find unattractive. (DiMaggio 1990, p. 126)

As the concept of social class becomes more fluid, stylistic innovations that connote upper class membership filter down to individuals from the middle classes. To maintain status differentials in an era where popular culture may overstep these boundaries, requires the consumption of goods which do not filter so easily. These are goods and behaviors which are not immediately acquired but developed through large investments of knowledge or time.

Pierre Bourdieu's book *Distinction* (1984) examines the concept of 'cultural capital' as it relates to France. Cultural capital involves both a set of skills related to educational pedigree and resulting occupation as well as upbringing. Both are knowledge and time intensive and help serve to differentiate social classes in a more stable way.

Yet as the society increasingly uses educational attainment as the method of providing intraclass mobility, many consumption items related to it become elements of positional struggle (Hirsch 1977). People's efforts to better their lives relative to others and/or relative to their current situation lead to difficulties in the context of social scarcity. The society can only employ so many managers, offer only so many houses in spacious areas close to the city, etc. While the end desired for most people may be a good job or a better job for their children, people still face a socially imposed scarcity (as opposed to physical scarcity). While many of these positional goods are pricey, they often require one to develop cultural capital in order to eventually secure the resources to purchase them.

As positional goods convey social status, under conditions of consumerism, other material commodities rise in stature as a basis by which moral worth is measured relative to work, intellectual, or leisure activities. Certainly the elimination of labor-leisure choice plays a role in selecting commodities as the direction of social and personal development. Also a market economy's tendency toward instability of geographic location and urbanization, both highlighted by Veblen, suggest the nature of social relations become more display oriented. Simultaneously, breaking the link between what one produces and what one consumes provides far greater commodity choice. Finally, class and occupational mobility, individualism, and the lack of labor-leisure choice all combine to help develop and then frustrate some of our life plans. Certainly some consumption then becomes compensatory as the world of goods is not closed to us, the way some of our life plans are.

Matching theory to history: a stylized account

From February to April 1923, the *Ladies' Home Journal* (*LHJ*) ran a three part series entitled, 'Our Social Ladder Its Sound and Rotten Rungs' by Mrs. John King Van Rensselaer, a name with origins to the (pre-Anglo) Dutch settlers of New York City. She remarks that economic prominence has replaced family lines in dictating who is placed in the society pages of local newspapers. She mourns:

> New York society is a thing of the past. There remain only fragments of it today ... The distinction that New York has seen the rest of the nation is now witnessing. In the contest between wealth and blood, between the self-made millionaire and the aristocrat, the latter always succumbs eventually. (Van Rensselaer 1923b, p. 152)

Although aristocracy was based on wealth, within the context of a rigid class structure, wealth was accompanied by patrician lineage and rituals. Within this system women had fixed social positions determined by birth and men could change their social position only by marrying up or down (Van Rensselaer 1923a). Social change was relatively slow and the well-off founding families of many cities developed cultural rituals to distinguish themselves from others. Their patrician lineage meant their standing in society was not solely due to their efforts, but to their family.

Grant McCracken (1988) has made a similar point in noting the role of patina in such families, especially in pre-Elizabethan England. Patina represented those characteristics of age and decay which befell upon family heirlooms. The patina was cherished for it indicated that the family had been of social status for many generations. Patina could not be forged. Thus, new wealth was clearly distinguished from the old wealth. The consumption focus was upon the family with clear attention to both past generations and future ones. Even merchants eager to rise to nobility did so within this social structure where five generations were often necessary before true gentility could be bestowed upon a family. The importance was not to create ever larger amounts of wealth, but to maintain it across generations.

McCracken traces the downfall of patina to Queen Elizabeth's use of competitive consumption display within her royal court to force nobility to spend themselves toward poverty in order to retain her favor. In so doing, they prioritized themselves before their families and future generations. This expensive process enhanced the queen's power by impoverishing the nobility. Although an historical examination of Elizabethan England is beyond the present analysis, the notion of ideological change does connect McCracken's analysis and Van Rensselaer's concerns.

As social mobility increased along with the ideology of individualism, patina no longer can confer status in a general sense. Patina symbolizes the family, yet what social mobility and individualism require are status symbols which confer status on the person. The individual requires symbols of status which demonstrate his or her success, not that of the family. While patina can continue to demonstrate old versus new wealth, this process becomes fundamentally distorted as patina-plentiful antiques are purchased or new novelties are displayed. In either case, the historical connection with family is severed and replaced by the individual and the present.

However, McCracken draws no connection between individualized consumption and production, yet that link is precisely what is required to understand the changes described by Van Rensselaer.

What Van Rensselaer's comments suggest is that the transition from competitive capitalism to monopoly capitalism brings with it a nouveau riche who, in order to gain entry into elite circles, must, in effect, buy their way in. In so doing, they change the reproduction process of social elites.

Competitive capitalism could not survive as outlined theoretically in Marx (1967 [1867]). Likewise, historical evidence has shown that price competition destroys profits (for the oil industry see Yergin 1991) and the growth of national markets required greater capital and new more bureaucratic organizational structures (Chandler 1977). These changes necessitated the transformation of competitive capitalism to monopoly capitalism, but in so doing, this transition created great (new) wealth for a number of individuals (and their families).

Thus, Van Rensselaer (1923a) points out that, despite popular perceptions, of the most notable families in New York – the Vanderbilts, Astors, Morgans,

Davidsons, Belmonts, Vanderlips, Reeds, Villards, Goulds and Millses - only the Astors' prominence dates back to the Civil War.

The economic development of monopoly capitalism created new claimants for social supremacy, meaning that the role of family lineage would now be compromised to also embrace the triumph of the individual. However, since individual success was created at the helm of corporations by one's own individual accomplishments, status came to be defined by what one purchased with new money, rather than inherited heirlooms.

According to Van Rensselaer, the wealthy are envied by the poor, not just for their money, but for the social position it has brought them (1923c). In the context of capitalist development the process of social mobility creates the emulation desires of self-betterment found in the writings of Veblen.

Further evidence of a change in social class characteristics are found in Kyrk and Veblen, but also in a content analysis of a cartoon strip of the time, 'Sam and his Laugh' (Glasberg 1985). In this racist cartoon which appeared in 1905, an ape-figured African-American 'Sam' absorbs the social tensions created by the breakdown of class rigidity by breaking into uncontrollable laughter at social situations which either represent some holdover from the past or the introduction of something new.

In each comic, 'Sam' answers an ad for a job, is hired, and then is unceremoniously booted out when he cannot control his laughter at the social situation which appears before his eyes. Glasberg's content analysis seeks to determine what is so funny about the society being portrayed and why a black man must be a scape goat. He classifies the changes as breakdowns in cultural forms, breakdowns in social roles, and breakdowns of class relations. All of these changes are consistent with a rising capitalist class overtaking the aristocratic rigid structure of the society. The fact that a black man must represent the target for amusement at the change reflects, according to Glasberg, the severity of the change and the fact that society was disingenuous in accepting the change.

The changes in class structure and culture are also evident in the work of Jean Gordon and Jan MacArthur (1985) who, in noting the changing consumption norms, find that mass production in the nineteenth century United States made greater wealth available to middle and upper classes, yet the styles which were copied were primarily French aristocratic, showing an emulation model following from aristocratic standards.

In fact, technology plays an important role in the upward mobility which reinforces the notion of classlessness and importance of extrapersonal impressions. Technological improvements in housing made it appear possible that capitalism could overcome its class nature. The unprecedented improvements in living standards in the early twentieth century became the basis for the elusive 'American dream.' At the same time for those left out, the failure to adopt commodity devices exerted great pressure on them, making them feel inadequate.

Rapid technological improvements enabled people to enjoy amenities within their life spans that in their youth only the rich had enjoyed. Perhaps the greatest was indoor plumbing, but the same held true for electricity and automobiles.

George Vanderbilt's 1885 bathroom on Fifth Avenue anticipated the standard design of the twentieth century (Giedion 1948). Yet, at the time, most people in New York still had to haul their water (Strasser 1982).

Some people felt like millionaires as indoor plumbing became commonplace. Others no doubt felt deprived and inadequate with the growing affluence around them. The 1897 Sears catalog offered no bathtubs fit for plumbing fixtures, no flush toilets or urinals, and only kitchen sinks, but the 1908 catalog had a full line of plumbing equipment. By 1926 indoor plumbing was no longer a luxury in Zanesville, Ohio as 91 percent of homes had running water and 61 percent had indoor plumbing (Strasser 1982). Likewise, electricity and motor cars expanded throughout the population within a generation. In 1890 Robert and Helen Lynd's study of Muncie, Indiana (a.k.a. 'Middletown') found less than five percent of homes wired for electricity and very few had running water. By 1925, 99 percent were wired and three-quarters had running water (Matthews 1987). By broader measures which included the slower pace in rural areas, Ruth Cowan (1983) notes that in 1907 the first year for which data is available, eight percent of homes were wired for electricity. The spread of electricity was also accompanied by a dramatic fall in its price. In 1912 when electrification was approximately 16 percent, a kilowatt hour cost nine cents. By 1920 when 35 percent had electricity, the cost had dropped to seven and a half cents. In 1930 the figures had reached 68 percent and six cents. Yet total expenditure increased as kilowatts per consumer doubled in the eighteen years (Strasser 1982).

With the spread of electrification, home appliances proliferated. A study of 100 Ford employees in Detroit in 1929 found 98 owned electric irons, 80 owned electric sewing machines, 49 owned electric washing machines, and 21 owned electric vacuum cleaners (Matthews 1987).

Automobiles became more commonplace in the 1920s following Ford's introduction of the Model-T. The average price of Ford's cars fell from $950 in 1909 to $290 in 1924 (Matthaei 1982).

The Lynds estimated that in Muncie in the 1890s only 125 families owned a horse and buggy (all members of the elite). By 1923 there were 6,222 passenger cars in the city, one for every 6.1 people or 2 for every 3 families (Lynd and Lynd 1929).

Thus the material conditions of life improved greatly demonstrating that class differentials might be overcome by the merits of technology. Technology worked in a double progression, imploring people to seek better products, while cheapening the value of what they already possessed.

However, the surging role of commodities was also created by the tremendous increase in advertising. Prior to 1883, most advertising in print media resembled classified ads, usually small, innocuous, and partitioned to the back of the publication. In the 1870s *Scribner's* and *Harper's* began to offer special prices for whole page advertisements. However, the *Ladies' Home Journal* (*LHJ*) typified the new magazine when its founder, Cyrus H. K. Curtis, publisher of the *Saturday Evening Post*, set its subscription price at 50 cents a year, one-sixth of its nearest competitor *Godey's Lady's Book*. The *LHJ* accomplished this feat by doubling advertising space (Strasser 1989).

The new magazines relied on shorter pieces, and rather than presenting an openly biased perspective sought to appear objective. These magazines quickly surpassed the subscription levels of the older ones. Their audience was rooted in the middle class of larger cities with a population exceeding 10,000. However, these magazines did try to reach out to readers of all income levels (Wilson 1983, p. 44). In 1923 the *LHJ* still cost only 15 cents a month due to advertising subsidies. The Lynds in 1924 found circulation for the *Saturday Evening Post* and *LHJ* sixty times that of the older style magazines, *Harper's* and the *Century*.(Lynd and Lynd 1929).

As advertisements were half the content of these magazines, *The Nation* editorialized:

> the editorial policy of nearly all magazines we know is happily approximating the advertising policy. In a superb miscellaneousness, in timeliness, in direct and vociferous appeal to the reader, the editors are, after all, not lagging so much behind. (1905, pp. 409-410)

Overall, advertising expenditures in print media expanded 10 fold from 1867 to 1900 and again in 1900-1925 (Matthaei 1982)! According to the Lynds:

> Advertising is concentrating increasingly upon a type of copy aiming to make the reader emotionally uneasy, to bludgeon him with the fact that decent people don't live the way *he* does; *decent* people ride on balloon tires, have a second bathroom, and so on. This copy points an accusing

finger at the stenographer as she reads her *Motion Picture Magazine* and makes her acutely conscious of her unpolished finger nails, or of the worn place in the living room rug, and sends the housewife peering anxiously into the mirror to see if *her* wrinkles look like those that made Mrs. X - in the ad. 'Old at thirty-five' because she did not have a Leisure Hour electric washer. (1929, p. 82)

This change in advertising was significant as it represented a cultural acceptance of the open hocking of products - something which had been frowned upon only half a century earlier (Leach 1993). Advertising and social pressure had an effect as Stuart Chase notes in reviewing *Middletown*: 'Homes are mortgaged to buy a car ... Out of twenty-six families without bathroom facilities in the work-class group studied, twenty-one had automobiles' (1929, p. 489).

Conclusion

Historian T.J. Jackson Lears described the growth of consumerism as a dialectical relationship between the emotional needs of Americans and advertising strategies. The overall effect was to create a capitalist cultural hegemony with a secular basis. As demonstrated above, this change has occurred not due to the 'false consciousness' of workers, but as a rational response to the social and cultural pressures within a capitalist economic system. As such, these ideas are consistent with the theoretical work of Antonio Gramsci (1971):

Gramsci has all too often simply been absorbed into a perspective which attributes an all-powerful social control to ruling ideas, norms and practices. The result is to reinforce a sense of victimization. At the same time he is frequently used to legitimize an alternative which is offered to this dominant ideology: a romanticized popular culture. In fact, while asserting the importance of the ideas and views of the world held by the mass of the population, Gramsci is highly critical of popular culture. What he seeks to investigate are the contradictions within people's 'common sense', and their ability to select among elements of the hegemonic ideology. This ideology, he says, is complex and often contradictory. In order to understand the effects of ideology, he focuses on the relationship between people's material circumstances and social relations, and their ideas. (Sassoon 1987, pp. 19-20)

Gramsci asks *why* people accept particular ideas and then judges that acceptance must emanate from material conditions in everyday life which appear to validate them. He looks at how practices reinforce the dominant ideology, but also how practices contradict it both in common sense and in dominant ideas.

However, without questioning the veracity of the social process I have described, this chapter has largely followed a class analysis. As such, I have developed a class-based theory of consumption, which although more in-depthly pursued than other writers (e.g, Gorz 1989), shares with it a failure to incorporate gender in a meaningful way.

Although class analysis may provide a penetrating tool for analysis, in this case the complexity of the social processes involved requires that class be combined with gender. The lack of labor-leisure choice, which affects both rich and poor alike (except the unemployed who experience involuntary leisure), also restricts the time to shop. Although it may create consuming motivations, it also frustrates them by limiting one's time. However, capitalist development freed one group of women - upper and middle class women. Capitalist development supplanted their household duties, giving them the time and opportunity to define themselves through commodities. In the next chapter we will investigate the historical rise of mass consumption and the critical role gender exercises through class in that process.

4 The contradictory marriage of consumerism and the homemaker ideal

Introduction

The relationship between consumerism and patriarchy is problematic, as no research integrates the two in a manner such that a qualitative relationship between the two is developed. Critical links between the social structure and the use-values associated with consumerism and homemaking have remained underdeveloped. Bonnie Fox's (1980) dissertation, for instance, provides rich historical detail to demonstrate the rising materialism of capitalist society. However, she provides no broader theory of the existence of consumerism or how that interacted with the patriarchal use-values associated with home-making. From slightly different perspectives Heidi Hartmann (1974), Julie Matthaei (1982), Susan Strasser (1982), Ruth Cowan (1983), and Glenna Matthews (1987) have all contributed to the historical research on the role of women's labor through the course of capitalist development. Primarily, they seek to validate the work of women, while noting their struggles against subordination. However, the broader interplay of consumerism remains exogenous to their models and never fully interacts with patriarchy. Rather the transformation from a society which emphasizes homemaking as the proper role for women to one which requires wage work primarily occurs as a result of technological development and the absence of domestic servants.

They spend relatively little time developing this articulation between consumerism based use-values and patriarchal use-values such that women pursue the former as the ideal rather than the latter. Cowan, for instance, argues:

> Where the sociologists and economists have failed to find a casual connection, the historians may be able to suggest a substitute. The washing machine, the dishwasher, and the frozen meal have not been

causes of married women's participation in the workforce, but they have been *catalysts* of this participation ... Most American housewives did not enter the job market because they had an enormous amount of free time on their hands (although this may have been true in a few cases). Rather, American housewives discovered that, for one reason or another, they needed full-time employment; and subsequently, they discovered that, with the help of a dishwasher, a washing machine, and an occasional frozen dinner, they could undertake that employment without endangering their family's living standards. (1983, pp. 208-09)

Yet a specific analysis of the statement 'for one reason or another' was largely omitted from Cowan's work. I suggest that consumerism was instrumental both in homes acquiring electric commodity devices as well as the creation of inadequate income within those homes. Still, one must deal with the issue of class, as the first homes to acquire these gadgets were not the first ones to send their wives into the labor force. As Matthaei notes:

Equally central to the transformation of the homemaker from an ideal to 'just a housewife' has been the entrance of privileged homemakers into the labor force. Without this, the labor force participation of a married woman would have continued to represent the failure of her husband to provide for his family's needs: the homebound homemaker would have continued to represent the ideal woman. (1982, p. 274)

Matthaei introduces the important component of class. However, an intriguing paradox emerges from these analyses. Women who engaged in wage work preferred to stay home when wealthier women stayed home, yet when wealthier women engage in paid labor, they also prefer paid labor. This correlation suggests the importance of social stratification.

Fox (1980) provides rich historical data on the nature of women's work within the home and in the labor market and how income inadequacy based on budget studies and median male income might serve as a reason for women's movement into the labor market. However, she lacks a theoretical interplay between consumerism and patriarchy. For Fox, patriarchal relationships within the family have no role, other than making the wife the secondary wage earner. The process by which use-values are undermined within the home is left unexamined. The key implicit point of these analyses is that the patriarchal use-values associated with a housewife become superseded by the capitalist market use-values associated with consumerism. While I contend this transformation has occurred during the twentieth century, the overtaking has not been complete, as women still do most housework.

Chapters four and five aim to clarify this issue by focusing on how the materialism associated with capitalism influences the gender division of labor and creates strains leading toward the wife's labor force participation. In analyzing this situation two relevant variables will be examined besides gender: class and cohort. By class analysis I aim to focus on the segmentation of society and how women within households are situated with respect to both gender and class space. Although they share a common gender, when combined with class, differential behavior patterns occur. I will use three class designations: working class, middle class and upper class. I largely define these classes by the occupation of the husband. In this sense, I am following Talcott Parsons' notion that a wife derives her status from her husband. However, status-creation is more complex than that, as it is further dependent on the self-image of the wife and whether she accepts a subordinate and complementary function to her husband. Homemaking as an ideal must be integrated with familial patriarchy. Generally, sociological research supports a connection between the husband's placement within the social relations of capitalist production and the nature of the family's social stratification and perceived role for consumption. Hence, I will argue that the motivations for a working class wife to work are different from the middle class or upper class wife.

Working class wives will generally have husbands involved in blue collar labor or relatively menial service labor. In general, these positions tend to be more physically strenuous or mentally tedious and to lack promotion possibilities. By contrast, middle class husbands are more likely to be involved in management, education, or some other professional field where the job is more mentally challenging and/or offers real possibilities for upward mobility. Upper class husbands represent the top one to two percent of earners and will generally be concentrated in key positions within business corporations.

The upper class becomes the basis for emulation for two reasons. First, they have substantial financial resources compared to the rest of society. Second, the husbands and their wives sit in positions of economic and political power within the social establishment. Thus, the upper class has both money and power in a society that places great value on these traits.

The role assumed by upper class women represents the role model ideal for many working class and middle class women even though working and middle classes may perceive or interpret this role model differently. Whereas middle class wives more accurately mimic upper class behavior including out of home activities, working class wives overemphasize the external symbolic nature of the homemaker role model – housework (Collins 1991). These different interpretations of the role model ideal reflect features of their class position within the social structure.

In addition, the nature of the income constraint is much more real for working class wives. These households face a dilemma since they cannot have both a homemaker (to demonstrate the husband's family wage) and a wage earning wife (to improve their consumption standards); they must choose between the two.

Cohort effects relate to the different time periods in which women become socialized. As consumerism becomes ever more dominant, these values become especially reinforced in younger cohorts who develop a stronger inclination toward market work (Davis 1964; Moore and Hofferth 1979; Gerson 1985).

The rise of the first consumers: Victorian women

Since I have asserted that upper class women became the role models for other women, understanding the social process by which they became 'homemakers' is important, as consumerism was integrated in it.

Because of similar patterns of behavior and/or authors who carelessly apply the term middle class or upper-middle class, I will use the term middle/upper class in the historical section which follows. However, given the occupational characteristics of the labor force in the nineteenth century, the number of white collar positions were relatively few. Thus, even those who use middle class without defining it relative to an occupational base are most likely referring to those in the upper quintile of the income distribution.

Industrialization challenged the gender division of labor. When households were primarily rural, the home was both a consumption and production unit which required the labor of all occupants and included a gender division of labor.

Intriguingly, many of the early devices which 'improved' life in the household actually augmented the tasks of the wife, while liberating those of the husband. One of the earliest areas of manufacturing was not textiles, but flour production. Families typically had ground corn into cornmeal. Cornmeal then was combined with leavening agents such as eggs to produce corn bread or other quick breads. The task of transporting and grinding the grain fell to the husband, while cooking was the wife's responsibility.

In the early 1800s commercial mills, which provided flour on an increasingly cheaper basis, began to spring up. The average wholesale price of 100 pounds of flour fell from $8.48 in 1801-1805 to $5.36 in 1855-1860 (Cowan

1983). Commercial mills created white flour which was preferred to whole wheat flour created at local mills, as the removal of the nutritious germ and bran reduced spoilage. The declining price and saved male labor in transporting grain led households to substitute purchased flour for their own. In so doing, husbands were freed of a responsibility. As the wealthier households adopted white flour earliest, white flour became a status symbol. Its use was reserved for delicacies like pies, cakes and yeast breads. As white flour was more widely adopted, women began substituting white flour in their baking, yet this change drastically increased the time and skill needed. As one recipe noted, the cook was asked to beat eggs for a cake for 45 minutes. Similarly yeast breads require careful monitoring of the yeast culture throughout the four hour process as well as kneading, neither of these requirements held for quick breads. Thus, the change to white flour clearly increased the load of the housewife, while decreasing that of the husband (Cowan 1983). More importantly, we see how the top-down transmission of consumer standards can augment the load of lower class housewives, when the upper class surely had servants to perform these tasks.

While flour may have been the most demonstrative example of the interplay of early consumerism and a patriarchal division of labor, many other 'improvements' had questionable effects on women's labor. The move from fireplaces to more efficient wood-burning stoves largely saved the labor of men who cut and split the wood. Wives still had to deal with the heavy cast iron of the stoves while cooking. Cleaning the stove became even more important, as a dirty stove would begin to rust. Later improvements to coal left more soot for the wife, but totally freed the husband of any duty except earning money to buy the coal (Cowan 1983).

Manufacturers of pots, pans, and shoes all displaced male labor in the household. Thus, clearly the nineteenth century consumerism helped to displace male labor, making it increasingly possible and necessary for the man to work *outside* the home. Yet these advancements probably increased the burden on women, working to entrap them within the home. The greater burden primarily resulted from the greater energy needs of homes for cooking and heating and larger and more extensive cooking equipment. The sphere of women's work within the home expanded, while the source of energy became dirtier (coal), making the expanding role also more strenuous. As Ruth Cowan notes, 'small wonder, then, that so many people commented on the exhaustion and ill health of American women during the nineteenth century' (1983, p. 66).

However, strenuous work was not the only source of ill health. Women's work not only became more strenuous it lost social value, as work's worthiness increasingly was measured by access to money. The effects on middle/upper class women were more widely documented, even though middle/upper class women had servants to perform these chores. As capitalist development removed the husband from the home, upper class women in particular experienced depression due to the functional void created (Stephens 1985).

Barbara Ehrenreich and Deidre English describe the phenomena:

> In the second half of the nineteenth century the vague syndrome gripping middle- and upper-middle class women had become not so much a disease in the medical sense as a way of life. (1979, p. 105)

A well-known doctor of the time described the illness:

> The woman grows pale and thin, eats little, or if she eats does not profit by it. Everything wearies her – to sew, to write, to read, to walk – and by and by the sofa or the bed is her only comfort. Every effort is paid for dearly, and she describes herself as aching and sore, as sleeping ill, and as needing constant stimulation and endless tonic. (Mitchell 1877, pp.27-28 quoted in Stephens 1985, p. 6)

Author and social critic Charlotte Perkins Gilman also had a bout with this disease which became known as 'neurasthenia' and found her only cure was escaping a life where she was entrapped in a role of solely raising children.

If we think in terms of the functional requirements of people in society, then capitalist development undermined the role of women, especially wealthier women who found themselves increasingly isolated in the home. Although the family had a functional requirement as an intermediary institution between the individual and society, what occurs during the middle-late nineteenth century is the progressive undermining of women's role in that institution. Middle/upper class women increasingly found their labors less socially important. These women likely felt a loss of 'membership' in society with the dwindling of their functional roles (Merton 1968).

The decline in the importance of wealthy women within the home corresponded with a diminishing role for women in society that occurred during the same period. Despite expertise in midwifery, women were barred from the medical profession. Likewise, they were generally no longer found as printers, blacksmiths, arms-makers, or proprietors of small businesses. Widows, once thought to be a challenge to power with the association of widowhood with witchcraft and often able to run successful schools, inns, cooking or sewing businesses, were now considered for public charity (Douglas 1977; Amott and Matthaei 1996).

Wealthier women soon became the engines of the new consumer society through a complex process which redefined femininity and turned them into a focal point for consumption. With more time on their hands and being part of the literate population, these women took up reading. But unlike their mothers who may have read Biblical literature, these women turned to novels, often written by women for women. In the 1850s, the combined sales of well-known male authors: Hawthorne, Melville, Thoreau and Whitman did not equal the sales of the any single one of the more popular domestic novels written by women (Hart 1950).

Two themes develop in a cultural redefinition of femininity as seen through writings and the fictional literature of the era. Women are seen as increasingly maternal, caring, and the upholders of spiritual goodness. But women in novels are also seen as consumers (Douglas 1977).

Novels became the rage just prior to the time when advertising took off. We have an interesting parallel because both involve the imagination where the image is suggested to the reader.

The presumed wastefulness of novel reading expressed at the time suggests the lost functional role of middle/upper class women. Debates at the time often reversed cause and effect; novels were seen as breeding idleness rather than as a reaction to idleness. Among the concerns included idleness, passivity and loss of the ability to think. Protestant minister William Peabody discouraged his son from excessive novel reading: 'It is to the mind like drinking to the body: it intoxicates and destroys the power of the mind for any strong and useful exercise.' In another instance, Peabody proclaims that it is due to novel reading, 'that so few people *think*' (Douglas 1977, p. 114).

Many of these same concerns have been voiced about television, but they have also applied to the effect of advertising. Novel reading and advertising actually became joint activities. Novel reading did not generally take the form of books. Most popular novels, such as those by Catherine Beecher Stowe, appeared first in serial form in popular magazines. These magazines also were a vehicle for advertising. In addition, women's magazines were far more widely read than men's magazines. In 1860 when *Godey's Lady's Book* was in decline, it still claimed 150,000 subscribers compared to *Harper's*, the leading male publication which had 110,000. *Harper's*, founded in 1850, had advertising 'fashion plates' placed at the back of each issue, while *Godey's* interspersed small 'fashion plates' throughout their magazine (Douglas 1977).

Like advertising, fashion itself provided another link between women and the growing culture of consumption. Although middle/upper class women had lost formal power, in its stead they were recipients of great hospitality and adornment by male suitors. As Timothy Dwight, a well-known educator and writer of the time noted: 'girls are taught to regard dress as a momentous concern' (Calhoun 1918, pp. 236-37). 'The self-involved style by the Victorian lady – pinched waist, swelled bosom, and proliferating protrusion of looped skirts and lacy petticoats – both obligated and exaggerated the female body; it objectified and enforced the female function as euphemism' (Douglas 1977, p. 61).

Hence, through a complex gender-centered process, the idealized role of women moved in the direction of embracing a consumer society. The same changes which challenged the role of women in the homes also opened up new opportunities, shopping. Many wealthier women found new meaning with a life which evolved around the department stores of the major cities (Leach 1984).

The first major department stores began to appear around 1870, but had become major institutions by the 1890s. Diaries of middle/upper class women in the 1840s indicate a strong religious devotion. However fifty years later, middle/upper class women had moved their focus from production and religion to secular consumption. Department stores were anchoring institutions in this change. Consumption represented a method of individual expression and freedom from strict norms of behavior, according to historian William Leach (1984), implying that women ought to be served, rather than serve others. Customer-service amid elegance were central marketing themes in these huge stores.

Middle/upper class women's access to the public space was limited. While middle/upper class men were active in labor markets and had their own exclusive clubs, these women had nothing comparable until the department store. Here a woman's power much exceeded her power outside its walls. Women could count on valet parking, free delivery of packages, telephones, and waiting rooms for weary shoppers. Within some stores, one could also find a restaurant, post office, child care, playgrounds, along with public lectures and weekend children's theater (Benson 1986).

Department stores both reinforced a class character as well as suggesting the broad opportunity of a consumer society. Although nominally open to all, highly ornate design and display served primarily to tell working class women they did not belong. However, so as not to lose these customers, large department stores offered less stylish, cheaper merchandise in basements (Benson 1986).

However, department stores also fundamentally changed the nature of shopping. In earlier days, shopping provided an opportunity to socialize.

Hence, the goods purchased were often a means to an entirely different end (socializing). While department stores became meeting places that enabled women to maintain their social networks, the stores also turned the goods themselves into the pleasurable end:

> People could now come and go, to look and to dream, per chance to buy, and shopping became a new bourgeois leisure activity – a way of pleasantly passing time, like going to a play or visiting a museum. (Bowlby 1985, p. 4)

The stores turned mass produced commodities into ones which carried social meaning. This change was also significant due to the large population changes which were occurring in America's cities. Between 1850 and 1910, New York's population increased six-fold. Chicago's growth was even more stunning, from less than 40,000 to more than 2 million inhabitants! In such rapidly growing areas, social display likely reinforced the usefulness of consumption (Laerman 1993).

These changes helped transform American value systems and gender-identity in the context of patriarchal culture. Two main criticisms during that time represent the changing ideology. Some questioned the adoption of luxury and associated it with privilege and sin. Others followed the socialist labor theory and questioned the relative social importance of buying, rather than making (Gordon and McArthur 1985). These ideological changes taking place for middle/upper class women's function are captured in the writing of Harriet Beecher Stowe, who admired her mother and grandmother and wished: 'for the strength and ability to manage my household matters as my grandmother of notable memory managed hers'. Yet she feared: 'that those remarkable women of olden times are like the ancient painted glass – the art of making them is lost; my mother was less than her mother, and I am less than her' (Stowe 1896, p. 98 quoted in Gordon and McArthur 1985, p. 39). Stowe herself delighted in the pretty clothes and china of the new consumer culture.

The functional adjustment of women was not limited to shopping. Women's labors were redefined to provide greater social importance. The early years of the twentieth century witnessed the rise of home economics and efforts to make homemaking a profession, but again these changes were done *through consumption*. Home economists argued for rationalized consumption and personally gratifying consumption. The wife managed her house, but access to consumption goods and deriving self-satisfaction from them was still contingent on the acceptance of an ideology relating to her position vis a vis her husband. Under the new ideology the husband earned the money and the wife spent it.

In order to make housekeeping acceptable, it was tied to the broader materialist culture. Housekeeping focused on budgeting – which was tied to shopping. It was also built upon a capitalist business analogy – where the housewife was the manager of her own home. In addition, personal gratification through heightened social status was emphasized, rather than the drudgery associated with domestic work. These ideas enabled women to distinguish their labors from the work domestic servants had previously done for them.

In this sense, advertising and new household appliances were important ways of separating the newly-defined household tasks from those that might be done by servants. A 1917 General Electric ad referred to electricity as the 'electric servant' (Strasser 1982, pp. 76-77). Electricity promised to give every housewife a servant! Magazines like *Ladies' Home Journal* (*LHJ*) were particularly important in purveying advice to these women and became an important connector between the proponents of Home Economics and capitalist enterprise and the housewife.

The business analogy and the homemaker

The discipline of Home Economics emerged as a home version of Frederick Taylor's time motion studies in industry:

> Housekeeping is a many sided business calling for training in theory and practice for scientific management. It needs as varied qualities as any business known to human beings, and yet as things are now girls and women are getting only the most superficial and artificial training in it. *It needs to be formulated and professionalized* and every working girl rich or poor should be taught at least its principles: at the same time she should be taught its relation to all economic and social problems and in particular to the cost of living. (Tarbell 1913, p. 130, emphasis added)

Christine Frederick's columns spread this gospel to readers of *LHJ* beginning in 1912. Each article started with an industrial brick laying example where scientific management had improved efficiency. Frederick stressed these principles to all housewives, especially those lower class women who might not yet own electric commodity devices (and few did at that point). The greater efficiency gains from better planning and saved motion could offset the lack of ownership (Matthaei 1982).

Yet the business analogy was severely exaggerated and, as a result, house-keeping did not develop the same kind of efficiency as modern enterprise. Institutional economist Hazel Kyrk (1933) noted many flaws in the business analogy concept utilized by proponents of household management. The business analogy reversed ends and means. Whereas business uses expenditure as a means to the end of income (and profits), households use income as a means to maximize expenditure. Even in maximizing the end of expenditure, the housewife had no clear measuring rod like profits.

The differences did not stop there. Although businesses were generally large-scale and undifferentiated, households were small-scale and differentiated. Thus, economies of scale were greatly reduced.

In addition, there may have been gains to inefficiency for the housewife. A housewife did not gain more income for being efficient (except in shopping, but even here she may not control that savings). Thus, her share was not linked to her productivity – cooking better meals did not bring anything in return, especially if they were not appreciated. Likewise, she had little threat of being fired, as a divorce, which would be the equivalent of being fired, represented a cost to the employer (the husband). By contrast, most business employees are much more easily replaced.

Time spent in housework

Even if a housewife were more efficient, the question emerges as how that time would be utilized. Hazel Kyrk observed:

> We have shown a tendency to use the time freed by labor saving machinery not for more leisure, but for more goods or services of the same character. ... The invention of the washing machine has meant more washing, of the vacuum cleaner more cleaning, of new fuels and cooking equipment, more courses and more elaborately prepared food. (1933, p. 99)

Why did this occur? Many writers have noted that despite the capital investments in the household, that full-time housewives showed no reduction in total time spent within the home (Vanek 1973; Cowan 1983; Walker 1969). Although these appliances had some reduction in total time spent in housework, the actual reduction was replaced by increased work in other areas: namely transportation, shopping and family care.

The most comprehensive survey of time spent in homemaking was the dissertation of Joann Vanek (1973). Vanek was careful to include only diary tabulated results, as results based on recall are less accurate. Generally, diaries were tabulated for a week and a housewife would list all her activities. The first surveys largely involved rural households in the 1920s and early 1930s and were commissioned by the Bureau of Home Nutrition and Home Economics. The studies generally were not representative in that the skills required to complete the diaries, namely literacy, were not equally distributed through the population. Thus, the population for these studies tended to be somewhat wealthier and more educated than average. Due to funding through the Department of Agriculture, they also were primarily rural, so there is a relative paucity of urban-rural dichotomies. However, the focus on rural homemakers (both farm and nonfarm) may not upwardly bias the results, as no significant differences have appeared in time budget studies. Rural studies distinguished between housework and farm-related work, which generally represented ten hours additional per week. As will be noted below, evidence suggests that if anything wealthier full-time homemakers spent fewer hours working than did their less wealthy counterparts.

Consumerism actually worked to increase the hours of housewives according to the Bryn Mawr study. Published in 1945, *Women During and After the War* found that farm families spent 60.55 weekly hours in housekeeping activities, while non-farm rural, small city urban (under 100,000), and large city urban (over 100,000) households spent 64.09, 78.35 and 80.57 weekly hours, respectively. The report concluded that: 'as living standards grow higher and more appliances and services enter the home, women tend to spend more time on home activity' (quoted in Myrdal and Klein 1968 [1956], p. 36).

Although Stanley Lebergott (1987) has criticized these samples as being small and skewed toward the highly educated, the consistency of results over numerous studies and the fact that for homemakers education may be negatively correlated with hours make any biases of dubious worth. The primary evidence of how wealth affected hours comes from contrasting the numerous rural studies collected by Vanek with an urban one which focused on graduates of prestigious women's colleges. These women were certainly upper and upper-middle class and had much greater servant help. Total hours (including servant hours) in these homes was significantly larger than lower income homes of full-time homemakers, 80 to 61. However, the hours of homemakers in wealthier homes were less, 48 to approximately 52, and more focused on family care. This was true, even though the family size tended to be smaller in the urban sample (Hartmann 1974).

However, how hours were utilized did change. Lebergott (1987) focuses on food preparation and clean up as the primary area which declined as numerous activities within the home moved outside it such as baking bread.

Gilman's 1900 study and Leeds' 1914 study cite approximately 40 hours per week in food preparation and clean up, yet the rural studies of the 1920s find that this figure had diminished by 40 percent, due to the development of market substitutes for homemade food items. While hours may have declined from 1900 to 1914 based on these studies (from 80 to 60), total hours stabilized in comparing 1914 and the numerous studies of the 1920s. The stabilization resulted from a change in the emphasis of housekeeping from production to service (cleanliness) and the movement of laundry back into the home with automatic laundry machines (Hartmann 1974). For the next 50 years, although there is evidence that the distribution of those hours gradually changed to emphasize family care and shopping over cleaning and meal preparation, the hours are quite resistant to decrease.

Table 4.1
Ideal versus actual housekeeping hours

Task	1920 *LHJ* hours Machinery With	Without	Time budget studies (1) 1924-1928	(2) 1943	(3) 1953	(4) 1965	(5)
Food Prep. & Clean-up	38.0	51.75	23.5	21.2	28.8	19.8	16.0
Clothing & Linen Care	10.0	13.0	11.3	12.0	6.0	10.9	8.7
Home Care	6.8	7.5	9.6	9.4	13.2	11.0	10.2
Shopping & Planning	6.0	6.0	3.4	4.2	2.0	3.8	10.6
Family Care	NI	NI	3.9	4.7	6.5	7.3	9.7
TOTAL	60.8	78.25	51.7	51.5	56.5	52.8	55.4

NI = Not Included.

Sources: *LHJ* (Sept. 1920), Vanek (1973, pp. 94-96 - Table 3.5).

While the consistency of long hours seems indisputable, the gap between the number of hours for ideal and actual housekeeping may have closed. In 1920 the *Ladies' Home Journal* reported that a home with machinery could be managed in 60 hours per week compared to eighty hours for a home without machinery. The changes are depicted in Table 4.1.

Table 4.2
Homemaker weekly hours and household equipment ownership,
1926-27

Equipment	Equipment Ownership	
	Farm	Town & urban
	(288)	(154)
Electricity	28.1%	95.4%
Furnace	7.4	42.7
Modern Plumbing	37.6	84.1
Electric Iron	24.0	91.5
Motorized Sewing	2.1	22.7
Electric Vacuum	6.3	43.5
TOTAL	51.6	51.5

Number surveyed in parenthesis.

Source: Vanek (1973, p.129 - Table 4.9) based on Wilson (1929).

Despite excluding family care, the lower *LHJ* numbers are still nearly twenty percent greater than actual time budget studies conducted by the Bureau of Home Nutrition and Home Economics only a few years later. If we take the *LHJ* numbers as representing a standard, then the proliferation of electrical devices enabled women to better clean their homes, but did not save them any time. Time was saved in the area of food preparation with the use of market substitutes. However, machinery did not appear to have a significant impact on time spent on housework. The first column indicates the mean for 559 farm homemakers and the second numbers indicates the mean for 249 rural nonfarm homemakers. Total time spent is remarkably similar even though rural nonfarm homemakers likely had more 'labor-saving' devices.

Maud Wilson's (1929) comparison of farm with town and urban homemakers in Oregon found no difference in time spent by homemakers, even though almost all town families had electricity and plumbing while only a third of farm families did. Overall, Wilson found that well-equipped homemakers spent only one less hour per week than poorly-equipped ones (see Table 4.2).

Similar studies by Whittemore and Neil (1929) and Richardson (1933) failed to find a decrease in hours worked when combined with the ownership of various modern conveniences. These studies found no difference in washing time among those who owned an electric washing machine, owned a hand-powered one, or did not own one at all. Richardson also found no difference between households with and without running water, as well as no difference between those with and without a refrigerator. Richardson did find that having a sink with a drain saved six hours per week over those households which did not have one.

Thus, evidence indicates that total hours for homemakers remained the same despite *expectations* – at least early on – that they would decrease. Early advertisements plugged their time-saving aspects. However, this gradually changed perhaps in response to social concern over leisure (Strasser 1982). Hildegarde Kneeland's study in the 1920s confirmed that time in housework had not changed. But her article describing her survey, 'Is the Housewife a Lady of Leisure?', suggests an overall social climate expectation that these chores would be greatly reduced. In fact, in issues of *Survey* in 1926 and the *Annals of the American Academy of Political and Social Science* in 1929 devoted to women, many articles expressed an expectation of decreasing household responsibilities, leading more women to work, especially part-time:

> Increased leisure, the development of labor-saving devices, the decline of the patriarchical family and the urbanization of America, the high standard of living, the single wage instead of the family wage for the man of the family, are some of the factors propelling the married woman out of the home into the occupational world. ... Part-time work is particularly suited to married women. (Pruette 1929, pp. 301, 314)

Yet these expectations did not come to fruition for those women engaged in homemaking. Commodity devices improved a housewife's efficiency so that she raised her standards, rather than lessen her time. But why did standards rise?

The answer to heightened standards comes not from the greater cleaning capacity of mechanical devices, but from the patriarchal aspects of the society. While Kyrk (1933) notes that a stigma was attached to women who did not properly clean their house, her analysis merely describes rising standards. More recent works, like Cowan (1983), have also described, rather than providing theoretical explanations for this change. The question then remains why women failed to obtain greater leisure time – or to the degree they did, why it was redistributed back into the home?

In part the heightened standards represent a defensive posture by wives. Heightened standards must be seen as both a response to patriarchy and the overwork endemic to capitalist labor markets. Juliet Schor argues in her book, *The Overworked American* (1991), that although payment by the hour has superseded pay by the day that was common during the Industrial Revolution, long hours remained the norm. Factory production was accompanied by larger capital outlays in equipment. In the competitive atmosphere surrounding firms, such equipment remained profitable only so long as no competing firm had found more technically efficient equipment. Furthermore, the equipment may have been purchased by loan, meaning that part of the profits from the equipment would go to moneylenders. Both of these forces gave employers an incentive to keep the machinery in constant usage. Idle time meant lost money. Such a task is best carried out by a minimum of shifts with a maximum of hours, as it minimized workers and costs.

Yet with very low wages and long hours, workers gained little by working. High turnover allowed a constant movement of workers between factories. Henry Ford's introduction of the assembly line and the $5 day, when competitors paid only $2, revolutionized production by creating a more highly productive and stable work force (May 1982). While this improvement is often attributed to the technical nature of the assembly line determining the pace of work, Schor additionally emphasizes the economic rent of such a relatively high paying job, which increased the cost of job loss to Ford employees. As a result, they disciplined themselves and improved their productivity to protect their newly found relative economic well-being. All of these arguments are reinforced by the broader social developments elaborated in the previous chapter. Thus, longer hours became consistent with wage work.

Likewise, struggling to reach the top of the corporate ladder for professional men also involved long hours and a commitment to the corporation, while someone else, usually the wife, took care of the home (Hochschild 1989; Blair et al. 1997).

Schor extends her argument on longer hours to the household. She argues that despite labor saving devices, that household labor hours remain fairly constant. Schor attributes this constancy to rising social standards from the American work ethic. The social ethic implies that he or she who does not work is lazy. This ethic derives from Puritanism according to Schor. However, she does not deeply develop this argument. She primarily uses it as a further reason why women in the household or men who won eight-hour days chose further labor, heightened household standards for women and second jobs for men, instead of leisure. Yet to leave the argument at that level essentially restricts higher standards to being a cultural artifact.

One can move beyond culture to make four additional theoretical points regarding how a patriarchal social structure in which men lacked leisure, in turn, affected women. First, one can apply the economic rent argument to suggest that women increased their services in order to protect their access to the higher incomes which their husbands received and/or to keep their husbands in physical and mental condition to earn those incomes.

Second, the fact that long hours were the norm made it difficult for married women to find part-time work. Part-time work did not become a significant part of labor demand until after World War II (Goldin 1991). Thus, most women faced a rather dramatic trade-off between full-time work and full-time homemaking, especially with the declining ability to work out of the home for cash, such as by taking in laundry or boarders (Jenson 1980).

Third, Kyrk's stigma argument can be reversed. Kyrk had argued that a stigma was attached to not adequately cleaning a house. In point of fact, no one actually inspects that house, but visitors might note whether a wife had leisure time when her husband was working due to the frequency of visitors or other activities and might deduce that she was an inadequate housewife, if she had so much time.

Thus, an additional defensive measure is to not lower the norm time for housekeeping. Many housewives likely adopted a regimen which kept them within existing social norms. The statistics which compare differently equipped homes, having little effect on overall time spent on various tasks highlights the norm effect. Capital improvements in the home only created the possibility of less work time. The potential change was lessened by the strength of prevailing norms including the distribution of work time. Thus, standards would rise and gradually the work load would redistribute. In addition, the greater efficiency of well-equipped homes made it possible for women to better emulate the homekeeping standards of upper class women. While their house might not be as grandiose, it could be just as clean.

Fourth, Schor's analysis indicates that even if a housewife could garner additional leisure time through the use of vacuum cleaners and such, she could not share such leisure with her husband. When capital improvements made it possible for women to become more efficient within the home, the possibility of leisure (and concern that the housewife become a lady of leisure) develop. However, this leisure, should it have been realized, would have been accessible only to the wife. The husband could not give up his job; nor could they share wage work responsibilities, not only because of the lack of part-time employment, but also because discrimination within labor markets led to substantially lower female wages (Kessler-Harris 1982).

Within the social structure what methods of leisure consumption were available for women that would be consistent with their own personal development and maintaining family status? Certainly the temperance movement and the suffragette movement politically captivated some upper/middle class women, but generally the political corridors were not open to women and this display of power would not rest comfortably within the patriarchal home. As we will see, middle/upper class women did combine homemaking with club activities, but even here the club activities were always scheduled earlier enough to make sure a wife was home in plenty of time to prepare dinner (Palmer 1989).

These four reasons provided powerful incentives for women to increase their homemaking standards, especially as long as patriarchal home-based use-values were seen as important. However, heightened housekeeping standards could not remain independent of society's growing materialist emphasis. In the next section I will elaborate on the nature of housekeeping standards and how a broader consumer culture interacted with it, primarily through an historical content analysis of the *Ladies' Home Journal*.

Homemaking and consumerism: a look at the *Ladies' Home Journal*

The issue of consumption affected the presentation of homemaking in the leading women's magazines. The *Ladies' Home Journal* (*LHJ*) had the largest circulation during the period of this study. While its audience had significantly greater income than average (approximately 30 percent higher), it represented a vehicle by which housewives interacted with the larger society. The *LHJ* provided a source of tips and new information and worked toward making housekeeping scientific.

As life provided more choices for people, experts gained importance in terms of providing training, advice, etc. This change was further reinforced by the presence of new technology. Since a woman's role was to support her husband and children, secular experts offered advice on the best methods and reinforced the notion that responsibility for their success ultimately rested on her shoulders.

Magazines became an essential medium by which isolated female readers could consult experts. However, this type of interaction served to reinforce consumer tendencies and undermine the nonmonetary work of housewives. Thus, although an overt purpose of the *LHJ* was to build up homekeeping, it had a more subtle effect of helping to undermine it by emphasizing the great importance of market produced use-values over original home use-values.

Commodity devices transformed the nature of housework by reducing directly-produced items such as basic food items and clothing and moving women more in the service direction of home maintenance and childrearing. As the home became more of a consumer of market items, women could no longer rely on past ways taught by their mother, as their home (and kitchen) bore little resemblance to their mothers' homes with the introduction of new technology.

Magazines like *LHJ* sought to professionalize housekeeping. As noted earlier, home economist Christine Frederick's columns bought scientific efficiency to readers. The scientific aspect contrasted with the traditional and emphasized the modern nature of housekeeping. The *LHJ* even applied scientific principles to baking. Research in the proper cooking of muffins and cakes included how many strokes to turn the batter and were reported to readers through articles written by Ph.D.s (e.g., Hallidy and Noble 1930; Love 1930).

In September 1920, *LHJ* ran an article that captured both the dramatic severing with the past and the great promise electrical devices had for reducing housekeeping time. The story recounted a newly married wife for whom the husband had designed a new home. Since the wife was not to see the home until completion, he provided hints, such as there would be many servants. Knowing the great difficulty in obtaining servants, when the wife told other women, they became quite jealous. When the big day arrived, however, the poor wife was disappointed – not only did the house have no servants, but it had no kitchen! She was in tears, but still managed to giggle at the obvious oversight. However, the husband intervened to show her that what she mistook for his scientific laboratory was, in fact, her modern kitchen with numerous electric devices (McMahon 1920).

Besides this tale of new adventures with electricity, *LHJ* also sought to make electricity more accessible to its readers. Ethel R. Peyser's 'Housekeeping in the Little House' columns in May and June of 1923 advised women on the merits of wiring one's house for electricity and what type of machinery could be used to make electricity work for you. Her article included safety tips on locating outlets away from beds and furniture and factual information such as that unused outlets do not consume electricity. But her overall theme reinforced the commodity fetishism for electricity. 'Of course, it's a bit more expensive to wire an old house than it is to wire a new one, but the excess is not sufficient to keep you from introducing the *benevolent* electric current into your home' (emphasis added, 1923, p. 36).

Ladies Home Journal also bolstered the materialism of society through homemaking. In 1923 the *LHJ* included many articles which helped foster material possession under sections entitled 'Needlework', 'Fashions', 'For Children' and 'Household'. Many articles began by connecting a reader's possible social concern to a remedy to be found in the article, but with the effect of creating unease with one's current situation.

In February, 'Making over the Living Room' begins with: 'it is discouraging, but true, that so many fully furnished and completely equipped living rooms have something the matter with them' (1923, p. 26). In March, Antoinette Perrett talks about the latest change in homes – attached garages for motor cars. The article includes pictures of possible designs and safety tips, including the need for a firewall to separate it from the main house. All the homes pictured are quite elegant and appear to have at least 3,000 square feet, making them substantially larger than typical homes (1923).

The linkage between money saving ideas and material consumption is illustrated by 'Colonial Trays that You Can Paint'. Thus, even the possible creative activities of housewives were connected to a money-based standard of consumption, not usefulness. The opening of the article explicitly ties consumerist desires to the project. 'Many a housewife has passed an antique shop or an exclusive house-furnishing store and seen the alluring painted trays, without realizing that with a minimum of effort and expenditure she might become the possession of an equally interesting article' (1923, p. 62).

Color in *LHJ* was reserved almost exclusively for advertisements, especially full page advertisements which frequently bisected articles. The color grabbed the reader's attention, making it impossible for a reader *not* to interact with the advertisements. Almost any item one can imagine was advertised in *LHJ*, including items no longer advertised there like home building designs, as well as furniture, beauty products, food, soap, and automobiles.

Households were not only becoming more materialistic, but the nature and social relations of household tasks were fundamentally changed by consumerism. 'Increasingly, after the twenties, [housewives] would move from the isolation in their homes via isolation in their cars to the relatively impersonal supermarket, with its hygienically packaged goods' (Matthews 1987, p. 192).

These changes affected the consciousness and self-esteem of women. The escaping from the isolation of the home is the theme of F. Scott Fitzgerald's 'Imagination – and a Few Mothers' from the *LHJ* in 1923:

> The average home is a truly dull place. This is a platitude; it's so far taken for granted that it's the basis of much of our national humor. The desire of a man for the club and the wife for the movie – as Shelley did *not* put it – has recently been supplanted by the cry of the child for the moonlight ride. (1923, p. 28)

For a woman to be confined there was mentally debilitating according to Dr. Abraham Myerson's *Nervous Housewife* (1920). Myerson noted that housewives are uncomfortable and unhappy. Although feminist historian Glenna Matthews (1987) feels he tends to blame the victim, she believes he hits an important core notion. On the one hand, housework is menial like ditch digging, yet it also carries tremendous emotional baggage. From Myerson: 'In its aims and purposes housekeeping is the highest of professions; in its methods and techniques it ranks among the lowest of occupations' (1920, p. 77).

Myerson identified that housekeeping let the mind wander, leading to monotony, day dreaming and introspection. Household efficiency proponents like Christine Frederick who had urged standardizing tasks, missed the fact that such routinization lacked an intellectual component. Myerson in an *LHJ* article of 1930 lauds the pre-Freudian and pre-Watsonian days when Freud had not corroded the mutual attachment of mother to child or Watson destroyed the self-esteem of the mother. Matthews (1987) notes that if a clinician singled out the deskilling of housework as the cause of such misery, the impact on women is probably substantial – only diaries could tell more adequately.

Female consumers reinforced their own isolation through the ideological mask of consumerism. By minimizing their expenses on necessities, which the chain stores offered, they saved money for items for their own or family's gratification or status-seeking. Many of these consumer devices reinforced this isolation by further eliminating social relations. Electric dryers moved the entire laundry process inside the home and away from neighbors. Suburban developments moved women farther away from each other. Cars improved transit but eventually led to the demise of delivery boys and small stores where social relations extended beyond simple consumer-merchant exchanges.

Take for instance the rapid growth of A&P food markets. A&P had 585 stores in 1913, opened 1,600 more in 1914-15, opened 2,600 more by 1919 and started another 11,500 during the 1920s. They started out with small stores operated by one clerk 'cash and carry', meaning no delivery and low prices. In 1920s self-service grew as did combination stores which handled meat, produce and groceries. During the depression 'cheapy' supermarkets in vacant warehouses with low markups became popular. They featured drugs, auto accessories, clothing, hardware, soda fountains and food (Strasser 1982).

By 1947 even in the *LHJ* the underlying notion that housekeeping is boring had become widespread, although not always overtly stated. In April 'A Housewife Looks at Soap Opera', the author notes the utter mindlessness of housekeeping (Heath 1947). To keep her mind occupied during her fourteen hour a day job, she turns to radio (books get damaged due to hand tasks like cooking and ironing). Of the options on radio, music can not get her through 14 hours, news is too fragmented, and although how to shows are helpful, she can't write down recipes while doing other tasks – which leaves soap operas. Soap operas with their plot can engage the mind.

Although one could still find a romantic view of housekeeping in *LHJ*, the tasks romanticized were those which were unusual such as those found in Gladys Tuber's column, 'Diary of Domesticity'. As a rural housewife she frequently relates her activities to nature and the changing seasons and holidays. Her column chronicles spiffing up the house, dinner for guests, reminiscing about her youth, a dog having puppies and tips for housewives. In March Tuber says: 'people often talk about how dull housekeeping is, but it seems to me that, on the contrary, it is a constant adventure' (1947, p. 244). The examples she provides include refinishing old furniture, inventing a new recipe, and painting rooms bright colors. However, none of these activities are ordinary activities for housewives, but two of the three tie directly to material possessions as an area to focus the mind.

In May of 1947, Mary R. Pride of San Francisco writes to say she loves Tuber's column as they both share a love of cats and: 'Also, she makes the everyday tasks that every woman has to perform *seem* like fun, as they *should* be' (emphasis added). Again her choice of words suggests her reality does not quite match the romantic world of Gladys Tuber.

That same month *LHJ* featured an article that surveyed readers and their husbands on whether men or women lead harder lives. Women felt they lived a harder life by a 2:1 margin, while the men were evenly split. Among those citing women's harder role, 37 percent stressed the length and monotony of housework (Benson 1947).

Upper and middle class homemaking and its necessary complements: leisure and domestic service

The growing isolation of housekeeping created a potential for dissatisfaction, since women were restricted to homemaking. Thus, a leisure option became an essential escape for many women. The presence of domestic help enabled many upper class women to engage in leisure-time pursuits. True ladies of leisure, as Veblen noted, spent their leisure conspicuously, yet just like conspicuous consumption, conspicuous leisure cost money – to be conspicuous one had to have the money to be noticed. Thus, this leisure option actually was consistent with consumerism. Charitable endeavors were one way in which some women engaged in conspicuous leisure. The questionable purpose besides a socially condescending ostentatious display of these charitable activities was noted by social critic Stuart Chase. 'There is again the almost limitless damage that wealthy women can do when they give way to philanthropic yearnings ... We must distinguish between the woman who is neighbor to her community and the charity gadabout' (1926, p. 270).

Besides charitable activities, other club activities dominated much of the time of middle and upper class women. During the early part of this century, college educated women joined alumnae groups to share their homemaking experiences. These groups always met during the day and left sufficient time for women to arrive home to oversee the preparation of dinner (Palmer 1989). In this way, 'leisure' time was allocated to voluntary work that did not politically challenge men. The Lynds' (1929) study of Muncie, Indiana found that the number of adult social clubs had grown from 21 in 1890 to 129 in 1924, even though the population had grown less than four-fold. The broadening could be seen within clubs as well. An exclusive women's club with just 39 members in 1890 and 75 in 1920, had 168 by 1924. Thus, for the middle and upper class, club activities were a strong complement to homemaking.

Those women who were not involved in club activities, especially working class housewives, had no avenue to produce greater work than through raising standards of housekeeping (Collins 1991).

However, housekeeping coexisted within the realm of capitalist materialism. Housekeeping increasingly worked to stimulate ever greater consumption standards, creating tensions for the future viability of a nonincome producing spouse.

Strains in the homemaker ideal became evident as more high school and college educated women from the upper-middle class pursued both work and family. The wives of male educators appeared to be an early group which experienced a breakdown in the homemaker ideal. In 1926 only 1 in 5 public school teachers or administrators received an income of $1,800 or more (Williams 1929). Thus, by professional standards, their pay stood significantly below those of similar social stature.

A 1926-27 study of members of the American Association of University Women (AAUW) found that only 768 of 6,535 had worked (for pay) at some time after marriage. Considering the high social status of these women, the prevalence of the homemaker ideal was quite strong. The Lynds' study found similar results in 1925 with only 1 of 40 business class wives working in the previous five years, while 55 of 124 working class wives had worked (Lynd and Lynd 1929).

Table 4.3
Distribution of family income, 1929

Income	No. of Families in thousands	Percent at that level	Cumulative Percent
$0	120	0.4%	0.4%
1-499	1,982	7.2	7.6
500-999	3,797	13.8	21.4
1,000-1,499	5,754	21.0	42.4
1,500-1,999	4,701	17.1	59.5
2,000-2,499	3,204	11.6	71.2
2,500-2,999	1,988	7.2	78.4
3,000-3,499	1,447	5.3	83.7
3,500-3,999	993	3.6	87.3
4,000-4,499	718	2.6	89.9
4,500-4,999	514	1.9	91.8
5,000+	2,256	8.2	100.0

Source: Wandersee (1981, p. 10) based on data from Levin, Moulton and Warburton (1934, p. 54).

The AAUW study focused on the 568 of the 768 who had worked at some time during 1926-1927. However, not all 568 answered all questions; so only a limited number of respondents were available for each question (Woodhouse 1929). The median family income for the sample exceeded $5,000, roughly three times the national median. According to a Brookings Institute study on the distribution of family income in 1929, these families were in the upper ten percent of the distribution (see Table 4.3).[1]

The study found a significant over representation of wives of husbands in education among wives who worked (for pay). One-third of the husbands of the working wives were involved in the educational profession. Although this number included university faculty who were paid significantly better than those in the public schools, 1927 and 1928 studies of faculty at the University of California-Berkeley and Yale University, respectively, also found their pay lagged behind those of comparable social status, such as doctors and lawyers. These faculty groups sought to emulate what they conceived to be a professional living standard, but generally described their lack of resources as causing financial hardship (Henderson and Davie 1928; Peixotto 1927, both cited in Wandersee 1981).

In the AAUW study more than forty percent cited a financial motivation as the primary factor in their work decision and forty percent of the remainder cited finances as the second reason for their work decision. Hence, family finances played a part in the work decision of two-thirds of these upper-middle class women. A desire to pursue a career or a love of work was cited by one in four as a primary reason and fifteen percent of the remainder as a secondary cause. The final significant motivation related to the tedium of housework or excessive leisure which motivated approximately one in five (Woodhouse 1929).[2]

However, these women were not stuck in low paying clerical positions. Claudia Goldin's (1990) studies of clerical pay profiles for women found returns to experience significantly below men. The AAUW data does not support that result for this particular college-educated group, reflecting the high social stature of their vocations. Of the 568 working women, 495 had full-time jobs with a median experience of between five and ten years. They generally made two-thirds of what their husbands made and their pay kept pace with their husbands with additional years of experience, if the wife worked full-time. These women due to the pay profiles associated with their jobs, were not engaged in dead-end clerical work, but had careers of their own on par with their husbands.

But these women still needed to embrace the homemaker ideal. Two-thirds of these AAUW working women employed domestic servants. Half of these servants worked full-time in the household. Another study of self-described career women found 90 percent employed domestic help (Palmer 1989). Thus, the presence of domestic servants was critical for these women to bridge the homemaker ideal with a career. The lack of a part-time intermediary option for these women made domestic service critical, as a dual earner couple with no outside help was a recipe for disaster, noted Hildegarde Kneeland:

> 'Let her husband share the work with her', the feminist suggests. But quite aside from the possible undue optimism concerning the husband's acceptance of this plan, can we consider it as anything more than a temporary makeshift? Can we look forward with any satisfaction to a way of life in which husband and wife prepare a hasty breakfast before dashing off to work, and return at the end of the day to prepare dinner, wash dishes, and do the cleaning and laundering? Many of us have tried it. And it is not our idea of a satisfactory home life, even for the family without children.[3] (1929, p. 333)

Class divisions in homemaking erased: the rise of commodity devices and fall of domestic servants

The previous sections have suggested that while women were reinforced for identifying with the home that identification process coexisted with a world of material status and material self-image. Thus, a fundamental tension necessarily developed as the housewife's ability to create use-values became increasingly tied to access to exchange-value – something which housewives did not produce.

In many ways, the question is not what led women to enter the work force, as why the housewife ideal persisted as long as it did. Randall Collins (1991) suggests that the housewife provides status in the same way that commodities might. Thus, materialism is suppressed by the competing status claim of the full-time housewife. However, this status element takes on different characteristics across social classes, with middle/upper class women often procuring status through voluntary organizational memberships, while working-class wives procured status from simply being in the home. However, a key aspect of this difference in time allocation was the presence of domestics to aid in menial housekeeping.

The decline of the housekeeping ideal correlates with a decline in domestic servants, in part, because domestic servants supported the patriarchal use-values associated with a housewife. The patriarchal system provided use-values that were not interchangeable with the market in the sense that the work of a domestic enabled the wife to have more time to cater to the needs of her husband and family. The availability of domestic help increased and reinforced the patriarchal division of labor by enhancing the use-values obtained from patriarchy and providing a market replacement mechanism for menial household labor. Women without servants could only try to emulate wealthier households. The time constraints of less well-equipped homes left them unable to allocate as much time to direct personal services as wealthier wives. A clear status hierarchy developed: families with domestic help, families with a housewife, and families with a working (for pay) wife.

Table 4.4
Domestic servants per 1,000 families and households, 1900-1991

| Year | Servants per 1,000 | | |
	Families (Stigler)	Families (Census)	Households (Census)
1900	94.3	NA	98.9
1910	93.1	NA	91.4
1920	61.3	NA	57.9
1930	67.7	NA	66.8
1940	60.0	75.0	69.0
1950	NA	39.2	35.9
1960	NA	40.3	34.4
1970	NA	23.3	19.0
1991	NA	16.6	11.6

NA = Not Available.
Data source in parenthesis.

Sources: Stigler (1946), cited in Hartmann (1974, p. 171); U.S. Dept. of Commerce, Bureau of Census (1975, pp. 41,144); U.S. Dept. of Commerce, Bureau of Census (1993, pp. 55,428).

In the period prior to 1940, domestic help although in general decline was still abundant enough and homes were equipped differently enough so as to maintain status differences in housekeeping. Hartmann (1974) notes that during the period 1900-1930, servants increasingly disappeared from homes such that by the 1930s only upper class homes had live-in servants, and no more than the top quartile of homes had any appreciable servant help (see Table 4.4).

Of course, the statistics cited above are misleading as a servant could serve multiple homes. However, the relative presence of servants declined from the period after World War I onward, as reflected in the servant problem which emerged in the literature at that time (Strasser 1982). While the number of homes which had domestic service help is unclear, research does provide us a good idea of how many homes were *not* served. Nienburg's (1923) study of homemakers in Rochester, New York found only two percent of homes with live-in servants. After, subtracting out the number of live-in servants and assuming each of the remaining servants served one home a day, seven days a week, then three-fourths of homes would have had no domestic service (Nienburg 1923 cited in Hartmann 1974).

By contrast Forbes in 1937 surveyed their 17,000 subscribers and found no comparable shortage of servants. Nevertheless, finding adequate servants was the impetus for the article.

- 12 percent had three or more full-time servants.
- 21 percent had two full-time servants.
- 49 percent had one full-time servant.
- 9 percent had a part-time servant.
- 9 percent had no servant.
- Mean number of full-time servants = 1.3, assuming part-time is half-time and no more than 3 servants.

One might ask if servants were desired, why did their wages not rise significantly enough as to augment the supply? The low status of domestics meant that as soon as jobs which had greater freedom and/or lower hours became available women eschewed domestic service (Strasser 1982). While domestic service has been a source of employment for poor women, during the late nineteenth and early twentieth century it was also often used by native and especially foreign born single white women as an apprenticeship of sorts as they learned how to be homemakers upon marriage. These white women weren't necessarily desperately poor. Life as a domestic was often quite difficult with evening hours, being constantly on call, and chores that were never fully defined. Gail Laughton's study in 1901 found that domestics or former domestics attached a social stigma to the occupation that deprived them of their dignity. So strong was this belief that many women opted for lower paying factory jobs simply to have clearly defined free time, including evenings when they might attend amusements or working women's clubs (Strasser 1982).

With this decline in the prestige of domestic service and the opening up of other opportunities for single white women, domestic service was increasingly left to African-American women who were usually married. In 1900 one-third of domestics were African-American (predominately women). However, they were still outnumbered by native born white women. Yet over the next thirty years, while African-American women increased absolutely in the field, the number of white women declined by half (Amott and Matthaei 1996), and the total number of servants per 100 families dropped nearly 30 percent (see Table 4.4).

Table 4.5
Ownership of electrical commodity devices
(percent of households)

Device			Year		
Major Appliances	1912	1932	1953	1971	1987
Vacuum Cleaners	0	30	54	92	99
Washing Machines	0	27	73*	70	73
Refrigerators	0	12	82	99	100
Dishwashers	0	1	3	26	43
Minor Appliances					
Irons	0	65	82	100	NA
Toasters	0	27	65	93	NA
Coffeemakers	0	19	47	89	NA

NA = not available.
* 1960.

Sources: Lebergott (1976, p. 288); Lebergott (1993, pp. 112-113).

Thus, the continuing decline in domestic service after 1930 primarily reflected the departure of women of color – most notably African-American but also Chicana – from that occupation. The social stigma and ghettoization of domestic work served as serious impediments to improving the supply of domestics. Likewise, racial and ethnic discrimination worked on the demand side to curb wage improvements. Yet we should also keep in mind that if the help was important enough, households (and not necessarily just husbands) would have been willing to pay more for it. Hence, it appears that the demand for domestic service was fairly price elastic compared to the supply that was fairly inelastic.

Table 4.6
Time budget studies of household and homemaker hours,
historical time and class differences

Task	(1) 1924-28	(2) 1931	(3) 1924-28	(4)	(5)	(6) 1931	(7) 1965
Food Prep. & Clean-up	27.6	25.4	26.9	23.5	21.2	15.1	16.0
Clothing & Linen Care	12.3	13.0	13.1	11.3	12.0	7.9	8.7
Home Care	12.8	12.6	16.1	9.6	9.4	7.4	10.2
Shopping & Planning	3.7	4.6	8.1	3.4	4.2	7.9	10.6
Family Care	4.5	5.5	15.8	3.9	4.7	**9.8**	**9.7**
TOTAL	60.9	61.1	80.0	51.7	51.5	48.1	55.4

Source: Vanek (1978).

After World War II for middle and upper class women the task of housework became more strenuous (due to the absence of domestic help). Meanwhile, for many working class women it was becoming somewhat less strenuous (due to household appliances – see Table 4.5). For example, although 80 percent of affluent households had vacuum cleaners in 1926 (Cowan

1983), in subsequent years vacuums became commonplace. As a result, the time allocation within homes eventually lost any significant class character (Vanek 1978).

This loss of class character partly reflected the greater dispersion of time-altering household equipment after 1950 and the rising popular literature, leading mothers of all social classes to raise their babies on Dr. Spock's advice, for example. As an arena of dynamic competition, homemaking essentially ceased to be one where extrinsic motivators affected women's time allocation. Intrinsic motivators from women's own personal standards developed over years of practice were still present. Additional status improvements to the household through housework were essentially satiated, such that further improvements in household efficiency made the monetary option for wives more viable, as status differences in consumption remained.

Changes in the distribution of household tasks across social classes can be seen in Table 4.6. Columns one through three compare *total* hours in housework between rural farm and nonfarm Bureau of Nutrition Studies with a 1931 study of alumnae of elite women's colleges. Columns four through six provide data from the same survey for the homemaker's work distribution only. In addition, the more contemporary Robinson and Converse study of urban homemakers is added in column seven. The Robinson/Converse study suggests that women had essentially removed class distinctions from housekeeping, especially in the previously socially distinguishing category of family care (Vanek 1978). In 1965, housewives with a college education averaged less than thirty minutes more on housework per day than those with only a grade school education. By income, lower income housewives were within ten minutes of higher income housewives in childcare and slightly above them in housecare (Cowan 1983).

The decline of domestic service also reflected a rise in its relative price to mechanical substitutes, changing food technologies such as 'T.V. dinners' which emerged after World War II, and the failure of domestic servants' wages to gain on other female occupations.

In 1959, the Bureau of Labor Statistics Consumer Expenditure Survey found 32 percent of households employed domestic servants at some time during the year, with an average expenditure of $196. Since the median income of domestics was $684, this expenditure implied that each domestic on average served slightly more than three homes. Previously Table 4.4 indicated approximately one servant for every 30 homes. These numbers suggest that domestics were dispersed between those serving only one or two homes and those serving a multitude of homes.

Table 4.7
Prices and expenditures for kitchen and household appliances relative to domestic service

	Year		
	1940	1950	1965
Price Ratio (1940=100)	100	63	31
Expenditure Ratio	0.33	1.09	2.23
	Percent spending of personal consumption		
On Domestic Service	2.76%	1.47%	0.78%
On Kitchen & Household Appliances	0.90	1.61	1.74
TOTAL	3.66	3.08	2.52

Source: Bowen and Finegan (1969, p. 232) from data from National Income and Product Accounts.

Table 4.8
Estimated expenditures per $100 of consumption for domestic service and household appliances by social class

	Year					
	1940		1950		1965	
	Dom.	Appl.	Dom.	Appl.	Dom.	Appl.
Middle class	5.28	0.78	2.33	1.43	1.19	1.56
Working class	0.88	0.99	0.39	1.83	0.20	2.00

Source: Table 4.7 and estimation method worked out in Appendix.

Yet expenditures for domestic service were in absolute and relative decline. From 1950 to 1965, while all personal consumption goods rose in price 31 percent, kitchen and household appliance prices declined 19 percent, but the cost of domestic service rose 66 percent. However, even with the price increases, full-year domestics gained no appreciable ground in comparison with other full-year female earners whose earnings moved up similarly (Bowen and Finegan 1969). Domestics still earned roughly one-third of the average female worker.

Not surprisingly, on an expenditure per $100 of consumption basis, expenditures on domestic service declined from $2.76 in 1940 to $1.47 in 1950 to $0.78 in 1965. Meanwhile, expenditures for kitchen and other household appliances rose from $0.90 to $1.60 to $1.74 in the same respective years. The changes are captured in the seven-fold relative expenditure gain for kitchen and household appliances from 1940-1965 relative to domestic service (see Table 4.7).

Based on the relative price changes (and if the appliances were a substitute for domestic service), one might expect a three-fold gain on appliances. Instead we see a seven-fold gain. This change reflects the much greater dispersion of appliance expenditure throughout the population (as noted in Table 4.5) as compared with a fairly concentrated expenditure for domestic service. Because real incomes are rising during this period, Table 4.8 indicates that across the time period the income elasticity of demand for housework related expenditures taken in the aggregate was less than one. But restricted to kitchen and household appliances, income elasticity was greater than one.[4]

The dispersion of appliances suggests that income elasticities were greater for working class than wealthier households. Although disaggregated figures are not available, one can surmise that the domestic servant effect is concentrated among middle and upper class households, such that these households largely decrease their relative spending on housework related expenditures (as defined above), while working class households maintained a fairly constant level of housework related expenditures. A hypothesized disaggregation follows (see Table 4.8). Since I did not have access to precise income class data for these categories prior to the 1972-73 consumer expenditure survey, I used data from the 1972-73, 1984 and 1991 consumer expenditure surveys. The data supports the general contention that on average working class households spent one-sixth as much per $100 of expenditures on domestic service as middle class households. On the other hand, for appliances working class households spent nearly 30 percent more on a relative basis than middle class households. With these adjustments, the income elasticity of demand for housework related expenditures for working class households exceeds one from 1940-1950 and equals one from 1950-1965, while the income elasticity of demand is substantially less than one for higher income households. This suggests that working class households were effective in improving their productivity relative to upper and middle class households, and as a result succeeded in eliminating class differentials in household services.

Once status differentials dwindled in homemaking, women found it more possible to trade-off homemaking activities for market work. In so doing, even full-time homemakers felt less social pressure to maintain extremely high standards. The use-values associated with the home had been surpassed in social importance by the use-values associated with the market, i.e., consumerism. With homemaking no longer able to contend with consumerism as a source of social status, increasing numbers of women entered wage work.

These changes can be demonstrated most dramatically in the falling burden of housework since the mid-1960s. The University of Michigan time use studies for 1965 and 1975 found full-time homemakers decreased their hours by approximately 5 hours (10 percent) per week. Overall, controlling for growing labor force participation and smaller family size, housework for all wives decreased by two and a half hours per week (Robinson 1980). These changes and the fact that the effect was greatest on full-time homemakers suggest the smaller macro pressure on full-time homemakers due to a lessened cultural status through meticulous homemaking.

However, despite falling hours, isolating work by the presence of commodity devices still did not significantly impact hours. The 1975 Michigan time use study data found when all other variables except ownership of household appliances were controlled for, only possessing a microwave oven showed a large time savings (70 minutes per week), but even this figure was not statistically significant. In fact, Robinson (1980) found no significant correlation with possession of any household device and time spent on housework. This result supports the contention that broader social pressures, rather than particular devices affect time spent on housework.

Buying patterns of households with and without a full-time homemaker

What evidence suggests that consumerism explains the growing movement of housewives into wage work? While surely not the only reason, consumerism does seem to be an important one. As women enter the labor force, the question arises as to how the additional money they earn would be spent. Do dual earning couples have different expenditure patterns than husband breadwinner couples? The issue is significant, because it relates to how rising living standards – made possible by a wife working – are actualized. Do women's earnings buy market substitutes for household labor in which case dual earner households should exhibit different patterns or do all households appear to follow a similar consumption patterns, suggesting other motivations for women working for pay? If consumerism is the motive, we would expect to see no significant difference between household expenditures by whether the wife works for pay beyond some modest attempts to purchase market substitutes.

Gary Becker theorizes that efficiency decisions motivate women's work. If this theory were true, women would replace their home labor with a market commodity version when they enter the work force. Hence, according to Becker, the spending patterns of husband breadwinner and dual earner households should differ in the areas of food and household maintenance and possibly time-saving appliances.

An alternative consumption pattern to Becker is suggested by Clair Brown (1985). Brown argues that the strong patterns of social emulation away from household related expenditures leads dual earner couples to not differ in their expenditure patterns than husband breadwinner couples of the same income. An implicit point of this analysis is that barring a redistribution of housework, working women endure the double day of wage and household labor.

Brown's data for household related expenditures for the 1950-1979 regressions uses a broader measure of household-related expenditures (HRE). Beyond food and clothing, appliances, semi-durable furnishings and auto repair are added. The regressions use macro time-series data, rather than individual budgets. The macro categories and very broad definition of HRE are problematic theoretically in terms of how such a wider measure is meaningful. For the time period, there were relative quantity gains in autos and parts, furniture and household appliances, and household operations and relative losses in food and clothing (Vickery 1979). Brown obtains a negative and significant relationship between HRE and women's labor force participation rates for 1955-1979. But the key factor is that relative budget allocations for food and clothing are just over half their 1950 level in 1980. This dramatic change more than compensates for the other subitems of HRE which increase. Thus, what her broader HRE figure and her negative relation between HRE and women's labor force participation captures is that food and clothing effect more than anything else.

The aggregate nature of her data make this a fairly weak empirical renunciation of Becker, since broader income growth patterns provide food with an income elasticity of less than one, even if within the macro-sample working wives spent considerably more on food. Thus, it remains possible that all food preparation could be done outside the home and the broad HRE figure would still decrease relative to other budgetary expenditures.

A more focused rebuttal to Becker is provided by Strober (1977), Strober and Weinberg (1980), Vickery (1979), Bellante and Foster (1984), Hanson and Ooms (1991), and Rubin and Riney (1995) who all found total family income and not the wife's employment is the primary determinant of expenditure patterns. All these studies used Consumer Expenditure Survey data, the earlier studies from 1972 to 1973, Hanson and Ooms from 1980 to 1983 and Rubin and Riney from 1972 to 1973 and 1984. All except Vickery and Hanson and Ooms applied regression analysis to the data to determine statistical significance.

Myra Strober (1977) rebutted Becker in finding that couples with working wives spent the same percent of their income on durables (such as appliances) as families with nonworking wives. However, possibly consistent with Becker, she also found working wife couples spent a higher portion of their income on consumption with no investment component (e.g., home expenditures are an investment). This consumption could include HRE. However, when Clair [Brown] Vickery (1979) compared expenditure patterns of working wife and husband breadwinner families she found that the source of income had no impact on budget decisions, except for extra work related expenses for the wife, e.g., clothing and transportation.

Myra Strober and Charles Weinberg conclude:

> Despite popular belief, working wives do not seem to use frozen foods or mail order catalogs any more frequently than do nonworking wives in the same income or life cycle. ... Although theory suggests that employed wives, who report greater time pressures than nonemployed wives, should more intensively use strategies to economize on time, we find that income and life-cycle stage are more salient determinents of time use than is employment status. (1980, p. 347)

Likewise, Don Bellante and Ann Foster (1984) found working-wife families did not substitute paid services (cleaning, laundering, cooking, and other domestic services) for work that would normally have been done in the home, if the wife was not employed.

Sandra Hanson and Theodora Ooms (1991) examined interview data for two-parent families with oldest children under 18. They found wives' employment led to increases in expenditures for food away from, domestic services (especially babysitting and day care), women's apparel, and transportation when families were compared on the basis of the husband's earnings. However, when total family income was compared (regardless of source), although families where the wives where involved in wage labor generally still outspent households where the wives were not employed, the differences diminished tremendously except for day care and baby sitting expense differentials which remained substantial.

In a similar vein, Rose Rubin and Bobye Riney conclude:

> At the same level of income, one-earner and dual-earner families have similar spending patterns, except for child care and transportation.
>
> It is notable that families of working wives do not use more domestic services than families of nonemployed wives. This suggests that differences in household production functions derive more from internal family substitution than from replacement of wives' housework with purchased services. Employed wives may simply reduce their leisure time (or sleep), or other family members may be doing more of the housework, or household standards may be lowered. (1995, p. 134)

This failure to more broadly purchase domestic services outside of child care counters the thrust of Becker's argument. From Becker's thesis, one would also have expected employed wives to be significantly more likely to use domestic help than households with similar income levels and full-time housewives.

These results are not unique to these data sets or the time period. Joann Vanek (1973) found in the time-use study of 1965 that households did not follow this pattern either. While families of low income levels were somewhat more likely to use paid domestic help, the differences were small (less than ten percent absolute difference). Those in the median income block ($7,500-10,000) and higher were no more likely to employ domestic help if the wife was working (for pay) than if she was not. Finally, where the wife was employed and family income exceeded $15,000, only 37 percent relied on routine domestic help (plus ten percent irregular domestic help), compared to 57 percent (plus 12 percent irregular domestic help) of similar income households where the wife was not employed.

Reorganizing Vanek's findings, we can compare households on the basis of nonwife (primarily husband's earnings) income (see Table 4.9). Based on Sweet's (1973) data from the 1960 census, this adjustment is fairly accurate. This adjustment provides a rough comparison of how much of the additional income generated from the wife was used for domestic help for a given level of nonwife income. In Table 4.9 it becomes evident that some portion of the wife's earnings in all categories was used to purchase domestic help. For employed wives, whose additional income pushes them above the median income threshold an additional one in seven (in nonwife income $7,500-10,000) purchased routine help when compared to wives whose income pushed their family into the median category. In the next highest income group that number increases to one in four (in nonwife income $10,000-15,000) who used routine (perhaps once a week) domestic help. However, nonemployed wives in the highest income category still used routine help more often than employed wives in the next highest income category. Hence, while there appears to be some income effect influencing demand for domestic service, the effect is by no means overwhelming. Rather domestic service was definitely a second priority to other material needs, especially in households with less than $10,000 total income.

Table 4.9
Frequency of use of paid help by employed and not employed married women by estimated nonwife income, 1965

Frequency of Paid Help

Nonwife Income (estimated)	Regular use		Irregular use		No use		Total		Number of Families	
	E	NE	E	NE	E	NE	E	NE	E	NE
< $4,000	.07	0	.08	0	.80	1.0	1.0	1.0	121	24
4-6,000	.08	0	.06	.08	.86	.92	1.0	1.0	48	50
6-7,500	.08	.01	.11	.08	.81	.91	1.0	1.0	64	77
7.5-10,000	.23	.08	.12	.13	.65	.79	1.0	1.0	68	75
10-15,000*	.37	.12	.17	.20	.46	.68	1.0	1.0	35	86
> 15,000	---	.57	---	.19	---	.24	---	1.0	---	37

E = Employed wife   NE = Not employed wife

* Households with employed wives and incomes above $15,000 are also included in the 'E' Column.

Source: Vanek (1973, p. 147 - Table 4.19).

Frank Stafford and Greg Duncan (1985) support this same point with their logit analysis of the 1975 Michigan time use data. The log of the hourly wage for married men – but not for married women – was a positive and statistically significant (at the ten percent level) predictor of the regular use of paid help. Furthermore, only seven percent of the dual income couples studied even employed regular domestic assistance.

A similar pattern appears in Hanson and Ooms (1991) for their previously mentioned study of two parent families with the oldest child under 18. When compared on the basis of family income, upper income households where the wife was at home spent four times as much ($436) annually on domestic service outside of babysitting and day care as upper income households where the wife was employed ($107). For middle and lower income families, wives employment status had no impact on these expenditures.

These results suggest that even when wives earn outside income, following broader cultural consumer aspirations and the double day of house and wage work are more consistent outcomes for women than using Becker's efficient labor allocation model. The persistence of housework suggests that status-enhancing or status-maintaining goods are being purchased instead of substitutes for women's home labor. We can conclude that women lack the power and or the desire to more forcefully replace their domestic labors. Examining the interaction of these forces is the topic for the next chapter.

Conclusion

The homemaker ideal was built upon consumerism, since the wife managed the purchasing, while the husband earned the money. However, to remain an acceptable occupation homemaking had to be distanced from the drudgery of domestic service. Thus, wealthier women isolated themselves from drudgery by employing and overseeing others to do much of the work. Since not all women could afford domestic help, homemaking became a method of social stratification.

In an era of the homemaker ideal, electrical devices only served to heighten standards of homemaking and had negligible effects on work load distribution. In the post World War II era, the growing presence of electrical devices for the home and a decline in domestic service exposed more wealthier women to the work experience of other women at the same time commodity devices enabled more women to improve their homemaking. The net effect was the removal of class differences in homemaking. However, it was not the inherent efficiency of commodity devices which lowered housekeeping time – but their socially determined intensity of use.

Hence, the patriarchal use-values associated with a housewife diminish both due to the shortage of domestic servants and the rising importance of market use-values. Evidence for the supremacy of consumerism over home-making related use-values is not only represented by rising labor force participation rates, but by consumer expenditure studies which indicate that women do not use their earnings to purchase complete market replacements for their labor. These results suggest the overwhelming importance of commodity purchasing which do not replace their home labor as a driving power in determining women's (paid) work decisions. However, the work decision is a function both of relative power in the family and the relative importance of commodities. The relative weight of these issues differ across social class. We turn to this issue in chapter five.

Notes

1. The Brookings figures were actually a composite of surveys, as there was no nationwide sample survey of family incomes in 1929. Instead, the Brookings Institution constructed a 1929 distribution for families and unattached individuals by combining a variety of different sets of income statistics for persons and then converting them to a family-unit basis. It may have been particularly inaccurate at the low end of the income distribution (Wandersee 1981).

2. There was only a 60 percent respondent rate for this question. The reasons for the other 40 percent are not known.

3. Given how this statement reflects life for many contemporary families, we can see how the relative importance on market-use values has supplanted those associated with the home.

4. The income elasticity is based on comparing expenditures in two categories to see whether they increase (elasticity greater than one), stay the same (elasticity equal one), or decline (elasticity less than one) across time, since real income is rising across time. I am using income elasticity in a nonstandard way. In this paragraph I am considering the US as one family. Later I take a particular family's relative income position and hold it constant across decades.

Obviously, if one were to consider moving up the relative income ladder, then one would expect income elasticities for domestic service to be greater than one.

5   Gender-identity versus consumption-identity: the battle at home

While consumerism has enhanced the power of women in marriage, the underlying persistence of patriarchy has both limited these gains and led to rising divorce rates.

When women enter the labor force, rarely do their husbands make significant additional contributions to homework in their absence. In fact, numerous studies find little (in magnitude, not necessarily statistical significance) or no correlation between the hours the husband contributes to housework and the wife's employment status. Studies generally find no more than a three hour increase per week in husband's domestic contributions when wives were employed as compared to husbands who were sole breadwinners (Hartmann 1981; Berk 1985; Coverman 1985; Pleck 1985; Blumstein and Schwartz 1991). As a result, women continue to bear primary responsibility for homework and childcare regardless of whether they engage in paid labor. This outcome clearly implies that something more than a simple consumption-identity is at stake here.

Arlie Hochschild (1989) argues that men and women develop a gender ideology as they grow up. For a woman it encompasses which sphere (home or labor market work) she wishes to identify with and how much power she desires to have in her marriage. A 'traditional' wife desires to identify with the home and be subservient to her husband. A 'traditional' husband holds the same views regarding his wife and identifies with monetarily providing for her. The 'egalitarian' wife desires to identify with the labor market and have equal power. An 'egalitarian' husbands shares these views. Finally, a 'transitional' wife seeks to identify in both spheres, but believes her husband should be more labor market oriented. Likewise, the 'transitional' husband supports his wife working, but believes she should have the main responsibility for the home. As a wife interacts with her husband each pursues a gender strategy aimed at securing these outcomes. However, what emerges is not a clear conclusion, but a multi-faceted interaction where marital power becomes quite important.

Rather than use Hochschild's 'ideology', I will use 'identity' to suggest that this gender role is important in determining what it means to be a woman or man to a particular spouse. Failure in a gender strategy may place a gender-identity at risk. I wish to contrast this with a 'consumption-identity', which describes how one uses commodities to construct a social identity. By this I am not concerned with the gender-typing of commodities themselves or the use of sex to sell them, but how commodities provide status and comfort to the household as a whole (and in particular the husband) through enhanced living standards.

Along these lines one can conceive of the homemaker-ideal period which began to seriously decline after 1960 as one in which husbands and wives generally shared 'traditional' views. Even when the wife worked, both held the goal of her becoming a homemaker. The power of women within marriage was limited, since both spouses believed the husband should be dominant. Thus, from 1920 to1960 divorce rates were fairly constant, increasing slightly from 1.6 to 2.2 divorces per 1000 population (U.S. Dept of Commerce 1975).

After 1960 the divorce rate jumps significantly, reaching 5.2 per 1000 population in 1980 before declining slightly to 4.7 in 1990 and 4.4 in 1995. However, the more recent decline is also accompanied by a parallel decline in the marriage rate (U.S. Dept. of Commerce 1997). Hence, whereas in 1960 an estimated 20 percent of marriages ended in divorce, by 1980, 45 percent did (Popenoe 1993). The decline of the homemaker ideal correlates with rising divorce rates because it freed women from their 'traditional' gender-identities more quickly than it did so for men. Likewise, the supremacy of consumerism as a means of status acquisition worked to further create uncomfortable tradeoffs between these two identities.

The underlying causes of divorce have remained complex with studies finding sometimes contradictory conclusions for large data sets. The gist of the evidence supports the suggestion that women's employment is linked to higher divorce rates. Most likely the linkage is due to less tangible relationship factors, not captured well in these studies (Greenstein 1990; White 1990). The key is understanding the dynamics underlying the wife's work decision and whether her employment and resulting income is perceived as a gift or burden by the husband (Hochshild 1989). That women enhance their power and reduce their proportion of time in housework in remarriages (Pyke 1994; Sullivan 1997), also suggests that consumerism has generally worked to enhance the power of women in marriages.

The lack of a male family wage: 1890-1940

When wives engaged in paid labor in the decades prior to the second World War, they were largely driven by income necessity – not social status. Absolute poverty was a primary concern. Noting diet deficiencies, Clair Brown (1987) has argued that absolute living standards were an important concern regarding family survival.

The homemaker ideal mitigated against an overzealous movement of married women into the work force. Any trend that may have started in the 1920s when the term 'business girl' began to appear in *Ladies'Home Journal* was interrupted by the severe economic disruption of the Great Depression which led to a political assault on married women's right to work, when so many male providers needed jobs (Goldin 1990).

Although urban wives increased their labor market participation during the first decades of the century (see chapter one), the increase was dampened by the homemaker ideal, whereby women fit into five strata:

i. homemaker with full-time servant help;
ii. homemaker with occasional servant help;
iii. homemaker with no servant help;
iv. working wife whose income earning activities were restricted to the home; and
v. working wife who earned income outside of the home.

As long as this stratum remained, moving up in economic status generally meant moving down in patriarchal provided use-value. Since women who worked outside the home generally earned twice as much as those who restricted their work to within the home (Goldin 1990), families made a trade-off in terms of whether and where the wife worked. The relative strength of patriarchally-derived status vis a vis materially-derived status kept women within the home. Generally, outside work was only sought by those married women who had no access to a male pay check or whose husband's earnings were at the bottom of the distribution.

Table 5.1 provides a 37-year analysis of the total real weekly earnings (including hour changes) and relative hours of full-time workers in all industries. While this sample includes some women, it is predominately male. The relative weakness of consumerism is evident in that 'leisure' increases predominated, while real earnings were relatively stagnant. This predominance of leisure is not to say that hourly earnings did not increase, but that full-time hours fell approximately as fast as real hourly earnings increased, yielding constant real incomes. This result implies the relative weakness of consumerism in the national mentality.

Table 5.1
Real weekly wages and weekly hours in all industry, 1890-1926

1890-99 = 100

Year	Wages	Hours	Year	Wages	Hours	Year	Wages	Hours
1890	98	101	1905	101	96	1920	103	87
1891	100	100	1906	101	95	1921	109	87
1892	100	100	1907	99	95	1922	114	87
1893	102	100	1908	102	95	1923	121	87
1894	102	100	1909	103	95	1924	123	86
1895	101	100	1910	99	84	1925	124	86
1896	100	100	1911	98	94	1926	125	86
1897	98	99	1912	100	93			
1898	99	99	1913	100	93			
1899	99	99	1914	100	92			
1900	98	99	1915	104	92			
1901	98	98	1916	104	92			
1902	98	97	1917	98	91			
1903	97	96	1918	100	90			
1904	99	96	1919	101	88			

Source: Douglas (1930, pp. 208, 211).

However, following World War I, this trend took a turn in an opposite direction as earnings increased faster than hours fell. This particular change coincided with the broader penetration of electricity into homes, following indoor plumbing (see Table 5.2). In addition, capitalists were successful in providing relatively inexpensive individual transportation with the automobile. As noted in chapter three, the Lynd's (1929) estimated that in Muncie of the 1890s only 125 families owned a horse and buggy (all members of the elite). By 1923 there were 6,222 passenger cars in the city, two for every three families.

Table 5.2
Homes wired for electricity

Year	Muncie, IN	United States (urban)	United States (all)
1890	< 5%	---	---
1907	---	---	8%
1917	---	47.4%	24.3
1925	99	69.5	53.2

Sources: Muncie: Lynd and Lynd (1929); U.S.: Cowan (1983).

Table 5.3
Growth of advertising

Year	Nominal	Real[1]	Real per Capita
1918	$1468 M	$1576 M	$4.77*
1928	3426 M	3426 M	9.22

M denotes million.
Real = 1929 dollars.
* 1919 figure .

Sources: Matthaei (1982); Douglas (1930).

By 1925 print advertisement expenditures were four times as large as 1900 in real terms. This increase was especially focused in the post-World War I years (see Table 5.3). The growth of consumerism did not yet fundamentally challenge the patriarchal division of labor due to the persistence of stratification among women. Thus, analyses of working women found without exception that employed wives either had husbands who were gravely ill, had deserted them, or made miserably low wages. Gwendolyn Hughes' (1929) study of Philadelphia families provides one example.

Hughes surveyed 12,000 families in the industrial working class sections of Philadelphia in 1918 and then conducted a more detailed analysis of 728 working mothers from that group. Among the larger group, she found that nearly half relied on more than one source of income. Wages from older children (18.6 percent) and wives (17.7 percent) were most common, followed by income from lodgers (15.9 percent). Only 7.5 percent relied on more than one of these supplemental sources of income.

The most common reason for mothers earning income related to the death, impending death, illness, or disappearance of the husband, which accounted for half of all working mothers. The other half worked primarily because of the inadequate earnings of the husband or unwillingness of the husband to adequately 'support me' (i.e., the wife), although 11 percent stated a preference for work. The clear connotation from this study was that absolute economic necessity determined whether mothers worked.

A 1925 study in Philadelphia also found a link between economic destitution and mothers' employment. Of 552 households that applied to the Family Society of Philadelphia for assistance, more than 80 percent had husbands earning less than the $38.15 per week judged as minimally adequate for a family of five (the approximate median family size for the sample). One hundred nineteen (22 percent) of the mothers worked for wages and an additional 81 (15 percent) earned income from caring for lodgers (DeScheweintz 1928). These numbers are significantly higher than the 24 percent of all urban married women previously estimated to have engaged in money earning activity (see Table 1.4).

However, the absolute minimum budget also provides an area where relative need can be seen. The $38.15 per week was devised by the Bureau of Municipal Research (B.M.R.), while the Family Society's own absolute minimum budget was only $22.57 per week. The B.M.R. was more generous in terms of rent, food, and utilities (including ice). The B.M.R. allocated $42 per month for rent, enough to buy slightly more than the 3/4 of a room per person, typical for five member families in the sample. While the Family Society allocated only $25 for rent, providing for no more than three rooms for a five member family. The food and utility budgets were twenty percent higher in the B.M.R. budget. However, these adjustments only cover half the difference. The remainder results from the complete omission of expenditures for transportation, education, recreation, household furnishings, club dues and taxes, health care, and miscellaneous others from the Family Society's budget (DeScheweintz 1928).

Many of these differences in budgets reflected areas of income elasticity that were the focus of growing consumerism. The Bureau of Labor Statistics conducted a cross-country study of 13,000 families in 71 large and 76 small cities with a family income range of $900-2500 in 1918-19 (Meeker 1919). The mode was $1350. The average was reported only as being a bit higher. Areas of high income elasticity included clothing, entertainment, and health care. Male adult clothing expenditure ranged from an average of $180 in the high income (not defined) group to $30 for the low income group. However, expenditures on clothes for wives were less than clothes for husbands until income exceeded $1800, suggesting women's clothing was highly socially stratified and very income elastic. Amusements were an area of surplus spending; as low income groups frequently spent less than a dollar per year, while high income groups spent nearly $40 per year.

A look at budget studies from that era back up the claim that husbands generally earned considerably less than what was judged to be the subsistence minimum for a family of five (see Table 5.4). The above mentioned 1925 B.M.R. and Family Society annual budgets are also found in Table 5.4. Almost without exception, the minimum budget stood significantly below mean male wages, whether the budget was based on actual working class budgets supplemented by expert opinion or estimated by experts based on local prices. Most working class households were struggling to attain these minimum standards, forcing many working class wives to earn money. However, as in Philadelphia for 1925, if we compare the budget figures for New York in 1914 to 1926 we note a $1,000 rise in the figures. If the level of necessities were fixed and the general consumer price index was used, the cost of living would have increased only $641. Although some of the differences could be explained by regional variation in prices, the large difference suggests that minimum standards increased – creeping consumerism.

The nature of pressures for rising standards can be seen in various studies. The 1907-08 Robert Coit Chapin study funded by Russell Sage Foundation excluded charity dependent families and limited observations to families with earned income and two spouses present. In New York and Chicago, he found 20 percent had bathrooms, 31 percent had toilets in their apartments, but only four percent of poorest income group had bathrooms. Yet by 1919 middle class expectations had trickled down to the poor. In the report prepared for Committee on Relief of the Chicago Council of Social Agencies, social worker Florence Nesbitt set a standard for sanitary facilities:

Table 5.4
Male wages, minimum budgets and family wage ratios, 1907-1927

Year	Mean Wage[2] $	Estimated Industrial Wage[3] $	Minimum Estimate $	Budget Actual $	Family Wage Ratio	Source (City)
1907	---	642		825	.78	Chapin (New York)
1908	---	636		675	.94	Howard (Buffalo)
1909	---	644		915	.70	Byington (Homestead)
1914	614	716		1070[a]	.67	Little & Cotton (Philadelphia)
				876	.82	Streightoff (New York)
				772	.93	Streightoff (Buffalo)
1915	606	727	845		.86	N.Y. Board of Estimate and Apportionment (New York)
1917	830	901		747[b]	.83	Mayor's Com. (Dallas)
1918	1080	1110		1637	.68	Bur. of Municipal Research (Philadelphia)
			1386		.80	Ogburn (New York)
1919	1242	1262		1803	.70	B.M.R. (Philadelphia)
			1268		.99	Nat'l. Industrial Conf. Board (Fall River)
1920	1376	1520		1988	.76	B.M.R. (Philadelphia) -N.I.C.B-
			1604		.95	(W. Hoboken, Union Hill)
			1526		.99	(Charlotte)
			1693		.90	(Cincinnati)
			1733		.88	(Worcester)
1921	1082	1374		1742	.79	B.M.R. (Philadelphia)
			2334		.59	Labor Bureau (New York)
			2067 to 2573		.59 to .67	Labor Bureau (10 cities)
1923	1361	1459	1854		.79	B.M.R. (Philadelphia)
1924	1336	1486	1921		.77	Lynds (Muncie, IN)

Table 5.4 Continued

Year	Mean Wage[2] $	Estimated Industrial Wage[3] $	Minimum Estimate $	Budget Actual $	Family Wage Ratio	Source (City)
1925	1402	1523	1984[c]		.77	B.M.R. (Philadelphia)
			1174[c]		1.30	Family Society (Philadelphia)
1926	1466	1555	1880		.83	N.I.C.B. (New York)
1927	1469	---	2884[d]		.54	Nat'l. War Labor Board (U.S. cities)

'Family Wage Ratio' is found by dividing the budget into the Mean Industrial Wage (the second and higher wage number).
[a] 'Fair minimum'
[b] 'Bare minimum'
[c] Itemized details presented in text.
[d] Includes new items: radio, automobile and telephone.

Sources: Fox (1980, pp. 432-436 – Tables 19 and 20); Douglas (1930, p. 210).

> There should be toilet facilities in good condition with a door which can be locked, for the use of the family alone; running water in at least one room in the house besides the toilet. A bath room is highly desirable and should be included whenever possible. (1919, p. 4)

The tremendous increase in living standards and the cost of living is further demonstrated by the more comfortable minimum estimated by the National War Labor Board in 1927 which included an automobile, a telephone and a radio and stood a full thousand dollars greater than the minimal standard estimated one year earlier (Fox 1980). As noted above, that prior year estimate itself had risen well-above inflation during the previous decade as well.

The evidence suggests that the gradual growth in consumerism blossomed in the 1920s. Consumer expenditures on durables and the use of debt finance both grew substantially. The percentage share of all commodities that were durables grew from 12.9 percent during 1909-18 to 20.2 percent during 1919-29 (Shaw 1947). Although installment buying was originally designed for auto dealers to allow auto factories to produce continuously, as auto buying was seasonal, installment buying soon spread as a method of deferring payment for consumers (Olney 1991).

Families reacted to the difficulties by making other income savings adjustments, rather than send wives out to work. The typical family size shrank considerably in the first three decades of the twentieth century. Census data indicates the average household size fell from 4.9 in 1890 to 4.3 in 1920, a decline of 15 percent. Women began bearing fewer children, had a larger percent survive, but moderated the overall size of their families. The birth rate of women 15-44 fell by one-third in the nineteenth century and continued its fall during the first three decades of the twentieth century. Given improvements in health care, women needed to have far fewer pregnancies to ensure the survival of their offspring. The additional cost of children in urban areas, compared to their income generating capacities in agriculture, led to both a declining birth rate and smaller families (Van Horn 1988). As life spans increased, greater potential time became available for work unrelated to childbearing.

Ironically, the period of the Great Depression tended to reinforce consumerism by reinforcing the attraction of money and the goods money could purchase. Unwanted leisure intensified linkages of status with work, wages and good. Unemployment undermined the value of free time because it interfered with the routines of public employment and private play. Time became an enemy rather than a goal (Cross 1993).

Income inadequacy and growing inequality after World War II

Rising incomes but still no family wage

As suggested by the growth of consumerism prior to World War II and the rising budgets of income adequacy, the upward ratcheting of decent living continued to undermine the adequacy of a male income in the decades following World War II. Had budgets continued to focus on meeting minimal needs, then a family wage would have been achieved. However, after the war, minimal budgets devised by the Bureau of Labor Statistics (BLS) focused on 'modest but adequate'. As such, they included car ownership and possession of household appliances, items not generally included in the budget studies of the 1920s.

To keep track of the cost of living in urban areas, the Bureau of Labor Statistics prepared occasional budgets from 1947 to 1976 based on a 'typical' family of four. The family consisted of a breadwinner husband, a homemaker wife, a son age 13, and a daughter age eight. The budgets were estimated for 34 cities from 1947 to 1951 and 20 cities beginning in 1966. The cities were spread across the country and varied in size, including all major cities as well as selected smaller cities such as Savannah, Georgia.

Table 5.5
Bureau of Labor Statistics modest budgets and male family wage

Year	Men's Mean Income	White Men's Median Income	Nonsubsistence Cost of Living (City Average)	Family Wage Ratios	
1947	$2,860	---	$3,300	.87	---
1949	3,225	---	3,519	.92	---
1950	3,461	$3,340[a]	3,718	.93	.90
1951	3,872	3,746[a]	4,166	.93	.90
1959	5,494	5,456	6,084	.84	.90
1966	---	7,164	9,049	---	.79
1967	---	7,512	9,076	---	.83
1976	---	14,136[b]	16,236	---	.87

[a] Series starts in 1955. Average ratio during 1955-1959 of full-time median to all earning median of 1.12 applied to latter category for estimate.

[b] Figure obtained for 1976 not separated by race. Figure is estimated using the 1970 income ratio of white men full-time to all men full-time applied to 1976.

Sources: For BLS Budgets: Kellogg and Brady (1948); Knapp (1951), Knapp (1952); Lamale and Stotz (1960); Groom (1967); Brackett (1969) and McCraw (1977). For Mean Wages: Fox (1980, pp.435-36 – Table 20). For Median Wages: U.S. Dept. of Commerce, Bureau of Census (1975, p. 305, 1977).

Table 5.5 compares these budgets with the mean of all men earning income and the median wage for white males working year-round full-time. In some instances, I have estimated the numbers to maintain a consistent string. In general, a gap develops in the family wage ratio which emerges in the mean in 1959 and the median in the mid-1960s. However, much of the gap disappears in 1976. Nonetheless, although in comparison to earlier budget studies, the men's wage may have made these budgets closer to a family wage, in no instance does median wage actually provide a family wage, even though in the defined BLS family the wife is presumed not to work.

Table 5.6
Growth of secondary earners to estimate BLS budgets in 1966 and 1976

1950:   Median Male Earnings = $ 3,340
1966-67: Median Male Earnings =   7,338
1976:   Median Male Earnings = 14,136

Nominal earnings factor increase 1950 to 1966 = 2.20
Nominal earnings factor increase 1950 to 1976 = 4.23

1950: Number of Families with two or more Earners: 39.1%
1965: Number of Families with two or more Earners: 48.7%
1976: Number of Families with two or more Earners: 54.0%

Estimated 1966 Modest Budget:
based on $3718 for 1950
($3718 x 2.2) + ($3718 x 0.096 x 0.33 x 2.2)= $8,439
Actual BLS 1966 Modest Budget = $9,100

Estimated 1976 Modest Budget:
($3718 x 4.23) + ($3718 x 0.149 x 0.33 x 4.23) = $16,500
Actual BLS 1976 Modest Budget = $16,236

Sources: For Two or More Earners Data: Vickery (1979), *Current Population Reports, P-60 Series*, no. 51 (p. 26) and no. 114 (p. 111), Table 5.5.

During this time period the number of employed wives increased tremendously and added to the family income. The 1960 Census one in a thousand sampling found 43.8 percent of all wives earned money income during the year. The range of their contribution ranged from 30 percent of family income for the typical employed wife of a husband who earned the median white male full-time income to 36 percent for the employed wife of a husband who earned two-thirds of the median and 23 percent for the employed wife of a husband who earned 50 percent more than the median (Sweet 1973).

Since male incomes continually rose in real terms during the period, an intriguing hypothesis is whether the growth in female contributions to income from rising participation rates reinforced economic need by further driving up BLS' modest but adequate budgets. This should not have occurred as this 'typical' BLS family had a full-time housewife. I have taken the 1950 budget as a base and then attempted to predict the 1966 and 1976 budgets on the basis of the growth of secondary earners in families. For simplicity, I have assumed that secondary earners' income increased at the same rate as median full-time white male income.

Consumer expenditure studies for 1972-73 found the typical working wife contributed approximately 25 percent of the family income or (assuming only wage and salary income) approximately one-third of what the husband contributed (Vickery 1979). Myra Strober (1977) using Michigan Survey Research Center data for 1968 finds a similar percentage. Thus, I have adjusted the 1950 budget by both an increase in median male wages and 0.33 times the additional number of households with two or more earners (see Table 5.6).

Intriguingly, the adjustment still falls short of the budget for 1966, although it slightly overstates the budget for 1976. In both cases, the adjustment procedure provides a more accurate estimate than if it were adjusted only for increases in median male white full-time income. This result supports the contention that growing female labor force participation had a social effect of increasing the definition of a modest budget, as families with working wives out earned families with a sole breadwinner (Bartlett and Poulton-Callahan 1982). Since the living standard is not determined by the male wage, but rather moves upward with the rising number of wage earners, a marginal effect on breadwinner husbands would be to place them into a relative budget deficit, creating further economic pressures for their wives to work.

Growing inequality

Deprivation pressures should be reinforced by growing inequality, both within cohorts with similar education as well as across them. Hence, growing male income inequality which has characterized much of the post-World War II era reinforced this relative deprivation. Claudia Goldin and Robert Margo (1992) assert that from the end of World War I to 1952 male wages compressed. Although census data was only available from 1940, pay ratios for skilled to unskilled workers in various occupations showed distinct downward momentum, with the only aberrant period being the later growth years of the 1920s and early years of the depression (1925-34).

Goldin and Margo utilized public use microdata samples (PUMS) from the 1940 and 1950 census and the public use sample from the 1960 census. The sample included white men, 18-64, who worked for at least half of minimum wage (not all men were covered by the law) on a full-time basis for at least forty weeks of the year. This definition would roughly coincide with that of a husband breadwinner. They found various measures which demonstrate a dramatic wage compression from 1940 to 1950 and a slight wage dispersion from 1950 to 1960.

Gary Burtless (1990) found greater inequality extending from the start of his sample in 1947 through 1987. Burtless used Current Population Survey (CPS) data for all male earners. Burtless excludes the top two percent of the earnings distribution to accommodate the earnings truncation ($50,000 for most of the period). He finds that the Gini coefficients increase for male earners in the 1950s from a low of 0.307 in 1951 to a high of 0.365 in 1958. This particular time period is where he finds the greatest growth in inequality.

Most measures of earnings dispersion for the 1960s indicate relatively little increase in earnings inequality for men (Henle and Ryscavage 1980; Burtless 1990; Goldin and Margo 1992; Katz and Murphy 1992). However, as we move to the 1970s, inequality rises. Since this time period also corresponds with the beginning of large demographic changes associated with the entrance of baby boomers into the work force and less experienced workers generally earn less than more experienced ones, one possible explanation for the shift would be that the large growth in younger men increased inequality – an effect only felt across cohorts, not within them.

Numerous researchers have controlled for education and experience changes in the work force and all concluded that this factor did not explain the changing inequality. Martin Dooley and Peter Gottschalk (1982, 1984) used CPS data of male workers aged 16-62 who were year-round labor force participants. They note that the variance or inequality of log weekly wages and log annual earnings increased significantly from 1967-1978. They find the strongest trend toward inequality between 1967 and 1972, with inequality rising both between fixed education-experience level cohorts and within fixed education-experience level cohorts. One problem with this study is its exclusion of census non-reporters of income, which tend to be most common at the tails of the distribution, especially among higher earners. However, their inclusion would only increase the inequality trend.

Gary Burtless (1990) finds increasing inequality both within fixed education and experience distributions and between cohorts. Of particular note, he finds the nature of the inequality to be growing relative earnings of high earners compared to middle earners.

Lawrence Katz's and Kevin Murphy's (1992) findings also support the growing inequality during 1967-1977 period, both within fixed education-experience cohorts as well as between them. Katz and Murphy limit their analysis to full-time workers who worked at least 40 weeks during the year. They use CPS data and interpolate earnings for all truncated earnings at 1.45 times the truncated amount, their estimate of the average earnings of this group for the period.

Thus, a review of the earnings inequality literature demonstrates that, after a period of wage compression from 1920 to 1950, wage inequality increased during the 1950s. The period from 1958 to 1967 appears to be one of relative constancy in the distribution of male earnings, followed by significant increases in inequality from 1967 to 1977. This trend toward growing inequality has also continued since 1977 as well.

In general, this inequality is found both within fixed education-experience groupings as well as between them. This suggests that many working class households had relatively declining earnings, both with respect to their peer reference group and with respect to a college educated group with similar experience. These pressures likely contribute favorably to a wife's work decision.

Declining male working-class incomes

While inequality may be one factor, declining male wages certainly represent another. Since real wages for most working class men have remained constant or declined since the macroeconomy began to stagnate and then restructure after 1970, many working class wives were forced into wage work. Since 1970, growing inequality has combined with declining real wages – a correlation that did not exist in the 1950s or 1960s. The subjective choice for women to seek employment based on societal pressures around consumerism changed drastically as the number of good paying jobs for male working class breadwinners declined (leading to greater within age-education group inequality).

Keeping work experience levels constant, real weekly wages for men with a high school degree grew by nearly 20 percent from 1963-71. Despite stagnating real wages, they actually gained on the college educated in the 1970s. However, by 1987 they had lost nearly half of their real gains since 1963. When analyzed on the basis of years of experience, these losses were especially harsh on younger workers. From 1979-87 while male high school graduates with 26-30 years of experience lost two percent in real terms, those in the one to five years experience category lost 18 percent (Mishel and Frankel 1991). Other victims included those who lost their jobs through plant closings who frequently found re-employment in jobs that paid half as much (Bluestone and Harrison 1982).

The labor market increasingly favored those with college degrees (increasing inequality between age-education groups). As David Howell has argued: 'the most striking feature of the employment restructuring among male workers since 1973 has been less a shift away from low-skill jobs than the disappearance of high-wage low-skill jobs'[4] (Howell 1995). Thus, merely maintaining their current standard of living, especially with the price uncertainty of the 1970s and real wage losses of the 1980s, likely made the work decision a matter of compulsion, rather than choice.

Impact of married women on income distribution in husband-wife families

Given these inequalities, a further dynamic is how the labor force participation decision of women impacted the distribution of income among husband-wife families. Were working class wives effective in limiting this inequality?

Current Population Survey income distribution data from Robin Bartlett and Charles Poulton-Callahan (1982) suggest that the ratio of median earnings in families where only the husband earned to families where both the husband and wife earned fell slightly from .79 to .74 from 1951 to 1976. They found income to be more equally distributed in dual earner families than when the husband was the sole breadwinner.

The apparent paradox is that women's earnings display more inequality than men's (due to part-time and full-time work); so it seems odd that they would be the agents of equality. In fact, although women's aggregate labor force participation continued to be somewhat negatively related to her husband's income (O'Neil 1981), looking at marginal changes from 1960 to 1977, this was not the case. Paul Ryscavage (1979) indicates that 60 percent of the increase in employed wives from 1960 to 1977 came from working wives in the top 56 percent of all husband-wife households.

However, because the incomes of wives are not strongly correlated with their husband's income, working wives have the net effect of equalizing the distribution. The study by Carol Leon and Robert W. Bednarzik (1978) profiled part-time working women. They note that since 1950, over 40 percent of the jobs filled by women were part-time. More importantly they find a link between greater husband income and the likelihood of wives taking on part-time employment. This finding means that income from women's labors is less correlated with social class than men's labors, as most working class women are working longer hours (for lower wages), while middle and upper class women are more likely to be working fewer hours (but for higher wages). Phyllis Moen (1985) also found in her review of work patterns from 1972 to 1976, that while women's employment histories tend to be intermittent, for wives of professional husbands it is intermittent part-time work and wives of nonprofession husbands it is intermittent full-time employment. Hence, working class husbands have relatively more income added by their wives than did middle class husbands.

Thus, we now have a possible answer for why women entered the labor market – growing inequality. Working class wives enter the labor force for monetary reasons and hence seek full-time employment. As a result of their labor, their families were able to keep ahead of poorer families and not fall behind those above them.

However, by the 1980s this pattern had changed. Rebecca Blank's (1988) analysis of the 1985 Current Population Survey found husbands of working wives had higher incomes than husbands of full-time housewives. In addition, wives with greater education reaped the greatest real wage gains. The combined result was that from 1979 to 1987, wives in the top quintile of married couple families increased their real earnings by 52 percent, those in the middle quintile by 40 percent, and those in the lowest quintile by only 18 percent. Half of these gains come from women either entering the work force or expanding their work hours. Although the current trend is toward greater inequality, increased income from wives in the lowest quintile were still sufficient to just barely offset the real losses of their husbands on average (Mishel and Frankel 1991).

This positive impetus was further demonstrated by Sandra Hanson and Theodora Ooms (1991) who comparing how much of a wife's income represented a real gain when compared to families in which only the husband was employed. After deducting for work-related expenditures and taxes from the consumer expenditure survey for 1980-83, they found families with low income husbands experienced a 71 percent gain in 'leftover income' (income minus work-related expenditures and taxes) when the wife worked. Families with middle and upper income husbands experienced on average only 27 and eight percent gains, respectively. Thus, clearly, wives of low income husbands, had the most to gain financially by seeking wage work.

Consumption-homemaking trade-offs by social class

The decision for wives to engage in wage labor during the post-World War II years was then generally not dictated by absolute poverty, but the lure of attaining or maintaining a particular living standard through consumption. But the macro outcome hides the bargaining and tensions that occur within particular families. While the lost status of homemaking led middle class wives to move in the direction of wage work with more of a 'transitional' (part-time) orientation, working class spouses tend to be more 'traditional' in their gender-identities. Their 'traditional' orientation in part results from the constant struggle these families face to reach their desired living standards. Hence, they persist in the goal of achieving a homemaker ideal. Even though the homemaker ideal lost its status for middle and upper class women, it continued to hold the allure of many working class women. Thus, within this context the only women who would engage in paid labor would be those for which a consumption-identity has overtaken their gender-identity.

Sociological studies indicate that the process of emulation is expressed differently for working class households as compared to middle class households. Working class households appeared more eager to distance themselves from poverty, but are not as keen on emulating those above them due to a couple of factors. First, they were a bit intimidated by the cultural capital which these people possess or were perceived to possess (Rainwater, Coleman and Handel 1959; Sexton 1964; Cobb and Sennett 1973). Second, the nature of the husband's job led to a lower level of socio-economic gain. The life trajectory that is anticipated by working class households differ from that of the middle class. These households place a premium on acquiring household gadgets. Because these expenditures took away from money which could be used for housing, they were more willing to give up quality of residence in order to accomplish mere ownership with modern conveniences – as opposed to renting.

For working class households, commodities validate their existence in a way which the jobs of the husbands cannot. Some researchers have referred to this process as compensatory consumption (Chinoy 1952; Caplovitz 1964). Komarovsky's (1962) study of 58 working class suburban families in 1957 revealed the prevalence of a commodity culture, where consistently improving the living standard was particularly important.

Working class wives also differed from middle class wives in that they were much more isolated from the greater society, especially after a home was purchased. The working class wife's task was to clean the home, and she saw the home as the center of her universe. Unlike middle class wives, she was not busy running to club meetings and chauffeuring her kids around town. Hence, although she held much greater autonomy over her daily schedule, this autonomy came at the price of greater isolation.

These differences created dual motivations for working class women. In comparison to college educated women, housekeeping held higher status.

This result probably relates to the more menial work alternatives which these women faced (Bose 1980). They, therefore, were less distressed by home-making. On the other hand, they were far more willing to admit a need for money or a general yearning to escape the isolation of their home, as motivations for wage work (Komarovsky 1962).

The pressure toward wage work may be especially strong among home owners. Rainwater, Coleman and Handel (1959) suggest in comparing suburban working class and renter working class homes of equivalent incomes, that the former are much more likely than the latter to also own many other commodity devices. This result suggests that not only are these women more isolated, but they placed a greater premium on income earnings.

During the early post-World War II years, despite the significant growth of their husbands' earnings and the fact that many had family incomes above median family income, these women continually expressed a dissatisfaction with their ability to make ends meet. Part of this dissatisfaction reflected the economic uncertainty resulting from having a primary breadwinner who performed menial, low status labor.

Interviews of wives indicate that their isolation was further reinforced by an isolation with respect to their husbands. Often husbands did not share their leisure time activities with their wives, nor did many wives resent this. In fact, Rainwater et al. suggest that working class wives had a much greater tolerance for isolative behavior on the part of their husbands than middle class wives. Komarovsky (1962) interprets working class wives' tolerance as feeling that their husbands have earned the right to this behavior through their money-earning labor.

By contrast, middle class families were much more emulative of higher classes than seeking to distance themselves from lower classes. This attitude derived from the white collar occupation of the husband which had a particularly strong level of anticipated promotion. Thus, lower income situations were tolerated, and the wife worked in whatever ways to further the career of her husband. Middle class wives were much more involved in club activities and less likely to identify with the home; rather they tolerated the home. Their standards for cleanliness were weaker as they engaged in weekly cleaning, as opposed to a daily regimen (Collins 1991).

What is suggested by this depiction? The work choice for working class wives at one level is much more obvious, yet at the same time it is much more difficult. The level and immediacy of perceived income inadequacy is much greater for working class wives. In addition, their lack of club activities and feeling that they cannot afford to participate in them and/or the unstated idea of feeling inadequate to participate with those of a higher socio-economic class, means that their daily existence is also more tedious. Together these inadequacies suggest that finding wage work would be a particularly strong outcome.

Yet, at the same time, the psychic cost to the working class husband of having his wife earn money is certainly greater than the middle class husband, as it implies his inability to adequately provide for his family. Middle class husbands have status directly through their jobs regardless of whether their wives engaged in wage work, while working class husbands may derive status because their wife does not have to earn money. Thus, especially when children are at home, one would expect great resistance to wives' wage work. The outcome then is one where a tremendous tension within the working class household as patriarchy and consumerism intermix. The wife, in many ways, suffers from a loss of self-esteem and social importance, while also not finding adequate income to compensate for this difference. But, she also may be quite reluctant to challenge her husband by opting for a job. One way in which these competing desires were met is fashioned by one working class wife's fairly general sentiment as explained to sociologist Mirra Komarovsky in 1957:

> If a woman has very young children and goes to work, then that's for bread and butter and people might feel sorry for her. But if her children are older, say in the fifth grade or so, and she works part-time, they know it is just for extras, and that's nothing against the husband. (1962, p. 69)

For middle class wives, the issue of outside employment represents a possible substitute for club activities. Since club activities are associated with social class, it follows that the occupations that these women might seek must also be consistent with their social class. The occupational structure would be the critical component in determining whether middle class housewives would seek employment. Although surely some might take on 'working-class' jobs for the money, most would want to maintain social prestige as a white collar worker if they were working for pay. They might still cite economic reasons for working, but they are unlikely to take a job as a school cafeteria or factory worker to earn extra money (Oppenheimer 1977).

The tensions created within the middle class household would be different. Since the husband's self-worth would not be as tied to being able to support his wife, she would be much freer to move into the labor market, even though not as economically compelled to do so. However, this noneconomic reason creates problems within a materialistic culture, as economic necessity was often the only socially accepted reason for working (Oppenheimer 1970).

The middle class housewife views her own role more negatively than her working class counterpart, due to a greater qualitative difference in the nature of her job vis a vis her husband. Simultaneously, middle class wives face the important role of entertaining guests for their husbands and building strong relationships with those supervisors or co-workers who might aid in his promotion. Thus, even if she took an outside job, social pressures dictated that it still must come second to the immediate needs of her husband. However, the added income of the wife's job might be used to hire the appropriate help.

One method of testing the above depictions of social class motivations is provided by the 1955 'Study of the Growth of American Families' (Sobel 1964). Social class was not delineated in the analysis which I reviewed, but club attendance and education were — two items which correlate with social class. The interviews encompassed a stratified sample of 2,713 white married women of childbearing age, 18-39. Women currently wage working were asked to provide their main reason for engaging in wage work.

Reasons for wage working were classified into five areas: chronic or temporary financial problems, need to acquire assets, need to accomplish something outside the home, need to occupy time or meet people, and in the family business. Consumerism is most strongly suggested by the notion 'need to acquire assets'. However, what constitutes financial problems is also interwoven with the concept of financial need and could also connote consumerism. The need to accomplish something outside the home would describe the dissatisfaction with homemaking, most common among the middle class. Employment as a way to get out of the home should not be a main motivator for middle class wives who frequently escaped the home anyway, but could be one for isolated working class wives.

Table 5.7 represents the findings of the interviews for employed women only; as such it is a biased sample because only 29 percent of the sample was employed. Nonetheless, the table helps explain why these particular women chose to work for wages. Unfortunately, cross category tabulations were not possible from the data presented; so one can only surmise the social class characteristics from the data. The college educated women which would most strongly be categorized as middle class did find the highest percent of accomplishment seekers as expected. Likewise, grade school attendees, perhaps exclusively working class, had much stronger economic related motives for wage work. The isolation hypothesis does not find much support, as the only group expressing this as large motivator were wives of husbands with at least 50 percent greater than median incomes.

Table 5.7
Motivations for wage work by husband's income, club activities and wife's education

(Reasons by Percent)

	Reasons 1&2 'Consumerism'	Reason 3 'Accomplishment'	Reason 4 'Isolation'	No.
Husband's Income				
< $3,000	86	10	3	178
3 - 7,000	79	13	6	372
> 7,000	45	22	23	60
Club Activity (last 3 mos.)				
Belong				
Attended	71	17	8	228
Not Attend	78	11	7	73
Did Not Belong	81	10	6	346
Wife's Education				
Grade School	90	3	4	73
High School	78	11	8	478
College	61	28	6	98

Source: Sobol (1964, pp. 56-58).

In 1955 the median full-time income for white men was $4,458. Although the correlation between income and social class is not complete, one can see that apparently regardless of social class, even having substantially higher than median white male income did not preclude economic desires from entering the work decision. In fact, within the $3,000-$7,000 group, economic reasons were nearly as prominent in the top half of the income range as the bottom half, with 77 percent citing reasons 1 or 2 as their motivation for employment whose husbands earned $5,000-7,000.

One should temper these results by the impact of macrosocial pressures, which can be seen from public opinion attitudes toward wives' employment. When asked generically whether it is acceptable for a wife to work outside the home in 1936 half disapproved and three-fourths of those not directly disapproving gave conditional responses. A 1937 poll which added that the husband made enough to support the wife, found 82 percent disapproved of the wife working, suggesting that most of the 1936 conditional responses included some aspect of economic need (Oppenheimer 1970).

World War II's entrance of women into the labor market caused a significant growth in acceptance, which continued in subsequent years. A question in 1946 found nearly half of respondents supporting a wife with no children working if the husband did not earn enough. Approval only dropped ten percentage points if her husband did earn enough to support her – as long as she did not have children (Oppenheimer 1970). By 1960 approval rates for women's employment had increased somewhat as a general attitude toward wives working found 34 percent of husbands rating it a good thing. The positive attitude was much more common among husbands under 55 who were nearly twice as likely to approve (37 percent) as husbands over 55 (22 percent) (Morgan, Sirageldin and Baerwaldt 1966). Still these numbers pale in comparison to survey responses in the 1980s, where only 21 percent of men supported the notion that married women should not earn money if the husband could support her (Wilkie 1993).

These changing social sentiments suggested that men generally were becoming more transitional and less traditional in their gender identity. Yet given these reluctant social sentiments which still existed in 1960 toward outside employment, no doubt many women, especially those with higher incomes, may have felt particular pressure to identify an economic reason for working. The notion that material reasons supersede other reasons reflects a social preoccupation with the use-values associated with the market and a greater willingness (more predominant among women than men in the polls) to allow these values to surpass those associated with homemaking.

The change in social attitudes over two decades was reflected in another study. This cross-sectional study of primarily middle class (higher than average income) women was conducted by the Survey Research Center of the University of Michigan (Iglehart 1979). Comparing surveys two decades apart, 1957 and 1976, give some idea of changes in the attitudes of homemakers and wage working women. They surveyed 850 married women in 1957 and 616 married women in 1976. The responses to identical questions demonstrate a shift from family economic centricity to individual choice in framing housewife or work outside the home choices.

While the survey was not restricted to women of a particular social class, families with incomes higher than normal outnumbered low income families two to one in 1957 and nearly four to one in 1976. Middle income families shrunk from nearly half the sample in 1957 to one-third of the sample in 1976. This data suggests that results predominately represent changes within the middle class.

Of employed wives in 1957, 22 percent would have preferred to have been full-time housewives, while only three percent in 1976 expressed that preference. Those employed for noneconomic reasons (meaning they would work in the absence of financial need) outnumbered those employed for economic reasons 58 to 42 percent in 1957, but by 1976 the spread was 82 to 18 percent. When these answers were broken down to family income level, wage working wives in middle and high income households were especially driven by noneconomic reasons.

When women earning money in the absence of financial need (n=60 in 1957, n=183 in 1976) were further queried as to their motivations for working, a significant shift from 'Prevents negative state' (52 percent to 44 percent) to 'Ego satisfaction' (33 to 44 percent) occurs. This shift is consistent with the bored housewife hypothesis and the notion that women are becoming more career-centered in their labor market goals. Reinforcing this notion is that the jump came entirely from college educated women, while high school and less than high school remained consistent across the time period (see Table 5.8).

Among full-time housewives (n=627 in 1957, n=335 in 1976), there is a shift from a positive (68 to 50) toward a neutral or ambivalent (27 to 44) feeling toward their vocation. Further evidence of attitudinal change is seen in the future plans of housewives. Notably, one in six housewives surveyed in 1957 planned to engage in wage work in the future, while one in three did in 1976. Among those planning to find outside employment, one also sees a transfer from economic motivation to ego satisfaction from 1957 to 1976 with the former dropping from 59 to 49 percent and the latter rising 19 to 29 percent.[5]

Overall, the survey graphically demonstrates the decline of the homemaker ideal and how perceptions of housework became increasingly negative. But does declining economic necessity as a stated reason then mean consumerism is declining? No, rather income and consumption desires interact with the patriarchal structure of the home to challenge the power relations within it. As a result of changed power relations, women become freer to express attitudes regarding work that are similar to men. Economic necessity is a defensive response for wage work, as it essentially rationalizes one's deviance from the homemaker ideal. However, as the homemaker ideal faded and the use-values associated with homemaking fell in general social significance, women were freed to become much more career oriented. While many women who have unattractive jobs might still say they work for the money, many women in the middle class had careers where they could achieve a level of personal satisfaction no longer possible through homemaking. Still the existence of those jobs (the demand for their labor) was a result of the continued growth of consumerism within the general society.

Table 5.8
Ego-satisfaction as reason for employment by education, 1957 and 1976

Education	Percent of Wives Offering Ego-satisfaction as Reason for Working	
	1957	1976
< High School	30	38
High School	33	33
College	37	61

Source: Iglehart (1979, p. 38).

Gender-identity and the battle at home

The relationship of outside work to the power distribution within the marriage has been the subject of numerous studies. Ironically often the power distribution is at odds with the couple's espoused ideology. Most comparisons of working class and middle class college educated couples find a stronger belief in traditional sex roles within working class households than middle class ones (Rainwater et al. 1959; Komarovsky 1962). Others have noted the correlation with higher education and nontraditional sex role ideologies (Mason, Cazijka and Arber 1976; Vanek 1980). Intriguingly, by some measures power differentials are greater in the middle class households, perhaps due to the more superior earnings power of the husband. When power is measured in terms of who wins in decision-making when both spouses disagree, working women do better than nonworking women and working class working women do better than middle class working women. The general order finds rough equality between middle class money earners and working class housewives.

Of course, measuring a variable like marital power is troublesome as bias may be introduced by differing perceptions of husbands and wives. Sometimes only wives are interviewed. Other studies have used children as a possible independent determinator. Furthermore, respondents, while able to remember decisions may not remember who won in the decision or attribute power based on their own authority expectations. In other cases, the existence of power may suppress conflict that might emerge in a more egalitarian marriage (Komter 1989). Hence, power measurement is best seen as approximate (McDonald 1980).

Resource theory developed out of the work of Robert Blood and Donald Wolfe. They argued that material resources, not ideological beliefs, were the prime determinants of marital power. Blood and Wolfe (1960) studied 731 Detroit families for relative family power. They found a strong relationship between the husband's income and his relative power in decision-making in eight areas that involve interaction with institutions outside the family: husband's job, which car to buy, whether to buy insurance, where to vacation, house buying, decisions regarding a wife's work, calling which doctor when someone is sick, and how much money to spend on food (only wives were interviewed). On an eight point scale where husband dominance was highest at eight and equalitarian at four and lowest at zero, husbands earning less than $3,000 had a rating of 4.58, while those with incomes in excess of $10,000 had a rating of 5.83.

When income figures were more dispersed and husband's mean power was calculated for both high and low blue and white collar occupations, the results were not nearly as strong – indicating that income was the dominant predictor of husband's power. Therefore, it was not surprising to find that husbands whose wives were employed also had relatively less power than breadwinner husbands. In addition, they found a positive relationship between the length of time the wife had worked for wages since the marriage and her relative power.

David Heer (1963) studied middle and working class couples of Irish decent in Boston and lent further support to a gender-blind resource theory of marriage. The sample included families with at least one child in elementary school and a father between 26 and 46. Couples were interviewed together. Power was measured by husband and wife responses to the question: 'When there's a really important decision on which you two are likely to disagree, who usually wins out?' (1963, p. 255). Heer found wives of working class background exerted (statistically significant) more dominance than middle class wives, and working wives also significantly had greater power than full-time housewives. While greater middle class husband dominance in personal characteristics explained part of the difference, the remaining difference continued to be statistically significant.

In contrast to Blood and Wolfe and Heer, Lois Hoffman's (1963) study of Detroit families provides an example where ideology and power were measured with children as the arbitrators of who held power. Mothers were first questioned on their beliefs concerning a male dominance ideology, where women were subordinate to men. Children were then asked who does and who decides about each of 33 different activities. Hoffman found that among wives who endorsed male dominance and among those who completely rejected male dominance, working wives had significantly (at the five percent level) more power than nonworking wives. However, working wives who only partially rejected male dominance had less power than nonworking wives. Hoffman interprets her results as male dominance acting as a counterweight to the increase power potential resulting from a wife's income. Those women who only partially reject male dominance may seek to compensate for the threat of their employment by becoming less dominant. Those women who work and ascribe to male dominance because they are likely working out of economic necessity may see their husbands as failed breadwinners, 'and, therefore, undeserving of the deference due men in general' (1963, p. 228).

More recent studies have supported the general thrust of Hoffman's work, that having more material resources is not enough, if you are also the wife. While higher relative earnings give women greater voice in consumption matters, this does not transfer into the household division of labor – where outside employment decreases wives' hours by 15 to 20 hours weekly, but husbands' hours increase by approximately three (Hartmann 1981; Berk 1985; Coverman 1985; Pleck 1985; Blumstein and Schwartz 1991). One result is lower housekeeping standards, but generally it means the burden of the second shift disproportionately falls on the wives' shoulders.

However, measuring power gained by the division of labor is also problematic as it represents an arena where women do hold power. Thus, women sometimes cling to these tasks and merely wish that their husbands appreciate their efforts. If symbolic appreciation is not forthcoming, then wives are more likely to judge the division of labor as unfair (Berk 1985; Blair and Johnson 1992).

Even when husbands increase their involvement, they do it on a far more discretionary basis than do women, who usually retain tasks involving meal preparation and cleanup and childcare which need to be done on a routine basis (Berk 1985). Likewise, many wives resist their husbands' help because the husbands do a less adequate job, meaning they have to redo it anyway.

Both of these outcomes reflect a patriarchal gender formation as articulated through housework (Coleman 1991). Women maintain a power role in the home as largely a defensive posture in the marriage.

In general, working class households are more likely to have more egalitarian division of labors within the home, even though spouses hold more traditional views of the gender division of labor. This difference results from the more irregular workshifts of both spouses, meaning that they are less likely to jointly share paid workforce time and as a result some routine household responsibilities must be picked up the husband. Husbands may or may not resent that their wives work; and wives may or may not share this concern (Thompson and Walker 1989). In most instances economic necessity under the influence of consumerism drives these women into the work force.

The net effect of consumerism is to undermine traditional patriarchal roles and augment the relative power of the wife, but not in a consistent fashion. Husbands who are especially unsuccessful in their own careers and relative to their wives are more likely to engage in domestic violence against their spouses (Hornung, McCullough, and Sugimoto 1981; Thompson and Walker 1989). Thus, although earnings do position these women into a relative superior position, threats of physical or other kinds of abuse resulting from the lost self-esteem of the husband pressure her to adopt a more subservient role (Kurtz 1995). Thus, the net effect on marital power is mixed. However, the marriages that endure are ones which become more egalitarian, suggesting that consumerism does have the long-term effect of partially undermining patriarchy (Pyke 1994). Yet the difficulty of engaging in wage labor, leads both spouses to value the homemaker ideal and the male family wage. Thus, although consumerism is an important motivator in keeping women employed, the failure of labor market participation to provide a sufficient nonmonetary reward, leaves both spouses harkening back to a preferred alternative. Yet at the same time consumption sacrifices relative to their peers and desires to provide for their children prevent them from making this commitment.

Middle and upper class families have a different dynamic. Consumerism has less of an immediate draw as careers provide greater fulfillment and status. Hence, the need to secure material consumption to signify rewards is less. On the other hand, this status is still necessarily translated into particular living standards requiring fairly high relative costs of living. Because the men in these families are more prosperous, but also less traditional in their gender-identity, these couples are typically less traditional in their ideological dispositions toward the division of labor. However, in practice because the earnings of these women are frequently less necessary and a smaller percentage of overall family income, husbands use their relative power to keep their wives disproportionately in the second shift (Blumstein and Schwartz 1991). The effect of gender-identity may be so strong as to force even comparatively more successful working wives back into the home when young children are present (Hochschild 1989).

Hence, consumerism in this context has on the one hand helped undermine traditional patriarchy and the status of being in the home, making it fairly desirous that women seek paid employment. Yet, paid employment often creates an ideological-practical divergence. While ideologies support the wives' choices, husbands frequently use power to block the true freedom that results from this. To the degree that households incur high fixed costs (e.g, mortgage payments), a wife's employment should lead to stronger relative power in the marriage and enhanced bargaining position. But conversely wives may find the attempts to find greater personal fulfillment undermined by their more powerful husbands. Although part-time employment (a transitional strategy) through the mid-1970s was highly correlated with husband's income and if he held a professional occupation (Leon and Bednarzik 1978; Moen 1985), research using data from 1976 to 1984 has not found such a clear correlation (Blank 1989). This change may suggest that wives needed full-time employment to secure sufficient bargaining power improvement. Yet this strategy may lead to a showdown resulting in retrenchment by the wife (including a move back to part-time employment), divorce, or a more egalitarian division of labor (Hochschild 1989). Ultimately who values or needs the marriage more, will determine this outcome (Pyke 1994). Thus, like the working class family, consumerism by hoisting high fixed costs upon the household enhance the ability of wives to enhance their comparative resources that they bring to the marriage. But the ties to consumerism are diminished here due to the alternative status elements from the job itself for the husband or both spouses. Thus, the role consumerism plays is less effective overall.

Women who succeed still may face the challenge of the second shift and find that even bringing relatively more financial resources to the marriage does not give them dominant power, if their husbands find their gender identity incongruent to their consumer identity. However, husbands whose consumer identity overrides their gender identity will see a wife's earnings as a gift. Thus, the crucial issue comes down to gender identity vs. consumer identity. If the husband's consumer identity outweighs the gender identity, a the necessary precondition for an egalitarian marriage is created. If it does not, then conflict erupts which may lead to marital dissolution. Thus, consumerism in middle class families undermines patriarchy but in a complex game-theoretic way.

Conclusion

In summary, working class women are more motivated by material deprivation than power in seeking money work. This idea is further reinforced by the fact that most jobs that these women might gain have lower status to them than that of homemaker (Bose 1980). The key predictor, then, of working class women's labor force participation would be the wage performance of their husbands and the relative pressure from deprivation caused by growing numbers of working class money earning wives. In the post-World War II period wage inequality deepened and the spread between husband-only earners and both husband and wife working increased. Their work decision helped close this income gap.

By contrast, relative power deprivation is a stronger motivator among middle class women. The issue of power is partly found in the lack of reaction to the feminist book published in 1941 and the large reaction to a similar one published 22 years later. Nobel laureate Pearl Buck's *Of Men and Women* anticipated many of the themes of Betty Friedan's *Feminine Mystique* some 20 years later. But the society at the time was not yet ready to grasp the ideas (Matthews 1987).

Subelements leading middle and upper class women to seek paid employment included the loss of domestic help. Domestic workers both alleviated the strain of home work, but they also formed a power relationship by which middle and upper class women exploited working class women (Palmer 1989). The post-war years saw the rapid diminishing of this source of help. Although relatively few women were strongly dependent on this labor, the marginal effect would be to place a number of wealthy women into a position of doing more housework herself or lowering standards – increasingly these women chose the latter and entered the labor force. This process inherently weakened the homemaker ideal for all social classes, especially middle class women who did not have access to paid help. These women could increasingly see the inherent advantages to a higher income and greater relative marital power. The popularity of the *Feminine Mystique* in the early 1960s should be seen as due to these social changes in the lives of these women.

However, the differential between ideology and practice also signals an inherent tension within these homes, where a more egalitarian ideology is not in fact practiced. This conflict no doubt created particular tensions that led many of these women to pursue a wage work. For these women, consumerism is probably not the dominant motivator to work, but it is complementary with their desire to gain relative power in the relationship.

When wives move from being outside the labor force to the double work-day, something is given up, namely the patriarchal service and/or the level of cleanliness of the home. Although the day does 'double', it becomes physically impossible to actually double time. Furthermore, the choice of market goods rather than direct substitution for household labor means the level of patriarchal service within the home suffers.

Notes

1. Real adjustments made with Douglas' (1930) CPI which does *not* include advertising except as a cost of production in consumer goods. Due to the large inflation (15 percent) between 1918 and 1919, the average price level between 1918 and 1919 was used when converting the $5.03 nominal figure to 1929 dollars.

2. Male Wage (the first wage number) is mean male wage for all male workers as reported in Fox (1980).

3. Industrial Wage (second wage number) equals mean weekly wage from Douglas (1930, p. 210) times 48 or roughly equivalent to a 7.7 percent rate of unemployment. Douglas does provide average annual earnings, which are about 20 percent less than the figures in the table. But these numbers include a few part-time male workers and lower paid women. Hence, the Industrial wage reported in the table should be interpreted as a more accurate measure of median earnings for fully employed working class husbands.

4. Howell defines low-skill jobs as positions requiring a high school degree or less. Furthermore, he finds that from 1975-1990, the number of young full-time low wage (1.5 times poverty wage) workers with at least some college has risen by 30 percent (14.1 to 18.5 percent of those employed). Likewise from 1976 to 1990, low wage employment grew as portion of total employment by nearly 10 percent, even though the number of workers in the labor force with a high school degree or less has declined by ten percent.

5. In both 1957 and 1976 19 percent said to prevent a negative state.

6   Conclusion: women's incomplete gains from consumerism

I have argued that the process by which women entered the labor market was not simply a matter of supply and demand, rather the process was premised upon consumerism and contingent upon the values of consumerism superceding those of familial patriarchy.

Many writers describe the push and pull of women into the labor market. Women were pushed by the increasing efficiency of their factors of production within the home. Greater efficiency decreased the amount of time needed for homemaking, while schools increasingly removed children from the home. As a result, the monetary value of a wife's time at home became less. Labor supply increased.

Likewise, women were pulled by relative labor shortages after World War II, especially in areas which women were most likely to be hired (clerical and service). Rising real wages for market work pulled women into market work. Labor demand increased.

By this account efficiency is the guiding rod for determining the labor force participation of women. However, this account is premised on the underlying supremacy of capitalist commodity use-values in social consciousness. This supremacy was not immediately achieved, but rather emerged as a result of an interaction with class and gender domination – not efficiency.

Rising consumerism occurred – not out of an innate desire for higher living standards – but out of a specific social structure. Capitalism structurally denied the working class the choice of work hours, limiting labor-leisure choice. In so doing, workers adopted the higher living standard logic as their best alternative under conditions of long hours. This perspective not only helped workers adapt to the social structure, but enabled the social structure to reproduce itself.

I suggest that consumerism required the further breakdown of class boundaries to take root in the essentially European culture present in the United States during the late nineteenth and early twentieth century. Aristocratic class boundaries separated classes in ways that could not be overcome by higher individual material living. An emphasis on family wealth and obtaining 'cultural capital' assured the aristocrats levels of differentiation beyond mere individual wealth. However, capitalism undermined this tradition by emphasizing individual wealth over family wealth – turning aristocratic reproduction on its head. Class boundaries at least nominally fell and 'classless' capitalist and worker classes arose.

The class distinction remained, but the notion of movement between classes emerged. In the American case this social mobility neatly dovetails with the broader sense of individual achievement and individual rights embodied in the culture.

Together this process enabled consumerism to develop in the United States. Without a leisure option, workers emulated the consumption patterns of those with higher incomes. Comparative consumption became an external measure of social differentiation.

However, it was not the only measure of social differentiation. A parallel system of differentiation existed within patriarchal use-values. Some women were forced to engage in market work merely to survive in urban areas. Other women could stay home while their husbands earned a 'family wage'. Among these latter women, some hired servants to perform the most menial chores, while others had to do those chores themselves. These dual systems of social differentiation, consumerism and the patriarchal family, were not entirely consistent with each other. Higher material living could be gained at the expense of losing a full-time homemaker to the labor market.

Here again the efficiency argument runs into difficulties, as efficiency implies that market substitutes for homemaking would be purchased before other items. Yet as I argued in chapter four this result is not the case. The supremacy of the values of consumerism over patriarchal homemaking can be seen in the disproportionate share of expenses devoted to areas outside of homemaking.

The decline of homemaking use-values could only occur once the social values associated with homemaking declined. This decline in part occurred due to the inability of wealthy women to continue to use domestic servants as the basis of social differentiation. In the context of rising material living and the difficulties domestic servants faced in terms of long hours (especially live-in domestics, see Strasser 1982), the supply of domestic servants fell and their wages failed to increase appreciably. Households found they were unwilling to raise their wages appreciably to maintain this differentiation. At the same time, working class housewives, through commodity purchases, were effective in reducing the status gap. As a result, more wealthy women were forced to do the dirty work. Some rebelled and moved into the labor force.

In chapter five, I suggested that part of the nature of this rebellion was linked to the dual gains which women found through labor market participation – higher marital power and higher living standards. Middle class women, in the context of a social ethos that suggested material need as the only valid reason for outside employment, turned consumerism into a rationale for wage work.

Working class women, with much greater relative needs and an eroding homemaker ideal, increasingly found their families losing ground relative to higher classes and to other working class families. This relative deprivation provided great impetus for working. Ironically, although many of these women felt their husbands should be breadwinners, they found the labor market performance of their husbands insufficient to meet their material desires. Thus, once the homemaker ideal began to decline, only the remnants of patriarchal ideologies held these women back from wage work. In most cases ideology proved little resistance to relative material deprivation.

However, the decline of the 'traditional' patriarchal family has not meant that women have been completely liberated. While we can safely state that consumerism has worked to diminish familial patriarchy as working women have become relatively more powerful, unequal burdens of housework continue to demonstrate continued inequality. Women may now be free to take on paid employment and have a stronger – or even dominant – voice in key decisions. However, they are still automatically allocated the primary role in housekeeping. Studies of homework still show that women bear the vast majority of the household duties, regardless of how egalitarian an ideology the couple espouses.

Although I have focused on the influence of consumerism within married couples, the analysis has been incomplete. The relative number and stability of married couples has certainly diminished during this century. More than seventy years ago Beatrice Hinkle noted that marriage had been transformed from a matter of economic necessity to personal choice:

> For the first time in the history of mankind the economic condition is such that both men and women can consider their happiness and welfare as superior to the maintenance of the institution. (1926, p. 289)

Hinkle may have been a bit ahead of her time, but history has proven her assessment correct. While in 1960 nearly nine in ten families were married couples, by 1996 barely five in ten were (U.S. Dept. of Commerce 1975, 1997).

The decline of marriage as an institution is an added complication of the decline of familial patriarchy. The rising possibility of divorce certainly gives women more incentive to obtain labor market experience. Likewise, labor market experience makes it easier for women to terminate marriages by giving them greater economic security outside the marriage. The job of housewife requires an employer (husband). However, the idea of women working for wages is now frequently no longer a choice. In that sense it represents a return to the urgent necessity-driven context of married working class women pursuing monetary incomes in the years prior to 1930.

Despite the perception that divorce is a middle-class phenomenon, divorce rates continue to be higher for working-class and poverty-level families (Kurtz 1995). Thus, the same financial pressures which might lead lower income wives to work also might lead to eventual divorce. These lower income family divorces are also more likely to result from 'hard living' and domestic violence as compared to the more judgmental perception 'personal dissatisfaction' which is more common among middle class divorces (Kurtz 1995).

Taken together we have a rather dangerous combination for working class families: growing consumerism, declining real wages, especially for men, and the resulting growth in divorce.

We now recognize how real wage growth is critical in a materialistic society. As that wage growth has stagnated for most of the labor force, consumerism has created new strains, which the continued pursuit of consumerism only exacerbates.

Labor rights (and wages) have declined as labor markets transcend the limits of national legislation. Those most strongly facing competition from cheaper sources (and the corporate power resulting from it) – working class men and women – have fared the worst. Worker-consumers, likewise, continue to enforce the most price-efficient method of capitalist control on their fellow workers through their buying habits. Unlike 1951-1976 when working wives helped equate the income distribution, working class working wives now struggle to just keep their family buying power constant (Mishel and Frankel 1991).

The power of consumerism has continued as advertising now reaches every aspect of our lives, even indoctrinating young children who are often unable to make the distinction been advertisements and educational material in their public schools (Hayes 1998).

Consumerism has reached a crisis. Political processes have broken down under the weight of a globalized economy and fragmented society, as each individual addresses his or her placement in the labor market and seeks an adequate standard of living. Those who have succeeded in a globalized consumer society, continue to do so, but they also exert the power to continue to make the society work in their interest. But in a global economy, the political processes do not yet exist to ensure that the economy works for a majority of the citizenry. It is therefore not surprising to witness falling political participation rates, as labor force participation rises.

Markets have become a means of domination. Today's politics argues for the virtues of the consumer as dictated by the capitalist market. Rising inequality is both a result of the market and of the breakdown of democratic participatory processes to counteract it. The deterioration of society is also characterized by a loss of social interactions, including diminishing families. Yet the same politicians who rightly point to cultural decline, also emphasize market responses, failing to understand the link between market domination and cultural decline.

As Robert Lane has argued:

> If the market has a destructive influence on friendship (and I now think it does), it must be through elevating instrumentalist and materialist values over social values, by eroding communities and neighborhoods, and by intermittently increasing the demand for overtime labor – as in the mid-1990s. (1994, p. 539)

Capitalist markets have developed consumerism and had the unintended effect of helping to liberate women. However, rising individualism has also made divorce more accepted, and financial strains for working-class families made divorce more likely. Many of these women escape marriages due to threats of physical violence only to find themselves in the economically vulnerable position of having to raise children on an inadequate income.

Likewise, for women not yet married, diminishing working class male income earning opportunities mean that the financial gains from marriage are often negative. Thus, we have seen large increases in births by unmarried women (Olsen 1994). Given these outcomes, it is perhaps not surprising that so much of our politics now looks nostalgically back to the early post-World War II years. However, until social movements and politicians come to understand how we arrived at our present predicament, the needs of women are likely to continue to be under served.

Appendix

Derivation of table 1.4 (reprinted below)

Table 1.4
Estimates of white nonfarm married women's labor force participation and money earning activities:1890 and 1930

(in percent)

1890	Cities	Towns	All urban
Adjusted Census	3.9	3.9	3.9
+Boarding	7.4 (16.0)	4.9 (10.6)	6.5 (14.1)
Total	11.3 (19.9)	8.8 (14.5)	10.4 (18.0)
1930			
Adjusted Census	10.2	10.2	10.2
+Boarding	4.7 (12.7)	3.1 (8.5)	4.2 (11.4)
Total	15.1 (24.1)	13.3 (20.3)	14.4 (23.0)

Figures in parentheses denote percent of *all* married white women earning income.

Cities are defined as having population greater than 25,000, while Towns had less than 25,000.

From Table 1.3, 2.6 percent of married white women were counted as gainfully employed by the census. However, Smuts (1960) has pointed out that only 23,000 of the four million (0.6 percent) married white women on farms were counted as employed. From data from Durand (1968 [1948]) and Vanek (1973), it appears that approximately 40 percent of the population lived on farms in 1890. Hence, we obtain the following algebraic equation for the number of nonfarm women who were officially counted as employed by the census: $(0.40 \times 0.006) + (0.60 \times \text{Nonfarm LFP}) = .026$. This equation yields an estimate for non-farm labor force participation of married white women of 3.9 percent. In the absence of additional data, I assume that the 3.9 percent also accurately represents both city and town urban married white women.

I then use Goldin's (1990) data for adjusting for the presence of boardinghouse keepers. I apply the same conversion principle as used in Table 1.2 based on Goldin's data for 1890. For cities greater than 25,000 population, Goldin suggests 16 percent of married women had this occupation $(.16 \times .46 = .074)$. For urban areas with less than 25,000 population, Goldin suggests that 10.6 percent were boardinghouse keepers, yielding an estimation of labor force participation of $.106 \times .46 = .049$. Finally, since approximately 64 percent of the urban population was in cities and 36 percent was in towns (Fox 1980), I take a weighted average of the results for the all urban figure.

For 1930 the same procedure is applied. I continue to assume that 0.6 percent of married white farm women were counted as gainfully employed. However, the number of rural farm wives is now 25 percent instead of 40 percent. The algebraic equation now becomes $(0.006 \times .25) + (\text{Nonfarm LFP} \times .75) = .098$, and Nonfarm LFP = 12.9 percent. However, a survey cited by Durand (1968 [1948]) and Goldin (1990) comparing the 1930 gainfully employed married female workers to the 1940 labor force participant definition found an overstatement in 1930 of 2.7 percent; so I subtract this and obtain 10.2 percent. Assuming this overstatement might carry-over to boarding housekeeping, we use the lower estimate conversion figure suggested by Goldin of .37 (rather than .46) for 1930.

In 1930 the census found that 11.4 percent of *all* urban households had boarders (Modell and Hareven 1973). Because this figure includes both cities and towns, I disaggregated it based on the assumption that the ratio of boarding between cities and towns remained the same from 1890 to 1930 $(.106/.16 = .66)$. In 1930 the urban population was 56 percent of the total population – 39 percent living in cities (greater than 25,000 pop.) and 17 percent living in towns (less than 25,000 pop.). Hence, I obtain the rate of city boarding as derived from the following equation: $[(.39 \times \text{ City Boarding}) +$

(.17 x .66 x City Boarding)] /.56 = .114, whereby City Boarding = 12.7 percent. Town Boarding = .66 x 12.7 percent = 8.5 percent. I then convert these into labor force participation estimates by multiplying by .37.

Derivation of table 4.8 (reprinted below)

Table 4.8
Estimated expenditures per $100 of consumption for domestic service and household appliances by social class

	Year					
	1940		1950		1965	
	Dom.	Appl.	Dom.	Appl.	Dom.	Appl.
Middle class	5.28	0.78	2.33	1.43	1.19	1.56
Working class	0.88	0.99	0.39	1.83	0.20	2.00

The data is based on the National Income and Product Accounts (NIPA). Thus, to split it into working and middle class divisions, I used the occupational tables to determine the percentage of males in the working class and middle class (which was combined with the upper class). I then used family income distributions, assuming that the working class represented the lower portion of the distribution, to determine how much of relative spending was contributed by each class. This information was calculated for 1940, 1950 and 1965 and summarized below. The percent of family income figures are assumed to be the weights of working class and middle class spending for the NIPA data.

The next process was to determine the relative difference in spending habits. The earliest data that I could obtain which delineated domestic service and household appliance expenditure was 1972-73. However, the 1972-73 data was flawed because it included domestic service in a residual category (U.S. Dept. of Labor, Bureau of Labor Statistics 1978). Hence, I supplemented that data with consumer expenditure survey information for 1984 and 1991 that had a separate category for domestic service. This data relayed relative expenditures on domestic service and household appliances in two broad categories: all urban consumers and clerical and wage consumers only. This division was useful, since clerical and wage consumers correspond with my definition of working class. I then determined from occupational tables that in 1990 42 percent of the male work force was working class and in terms of income, the working class had 30.2 percent (see Table A.1).

Table A.1
Distribution of male occupations and family income by social class

Breakdown of Male Occupations (% of Family Income)

Year	%Working Class		%Middle Class	
1940	83.4	(57.3)	16.6	(42.7)
1950	68.9	(44.3)	31.1	(55.7)
1965	65.3	(41.5)	34.7	(58.5)
1990	58.0	(30.2)	42.0	(69.8)

For 1940 income distribution data is based on highest quintile of families for 1950. Income distribution figures were not available for 1940. No adjustment was made for 16.6 percent as opposed to 20 percent on two grounds. First, income was more unequally distributed in 1940 than 1950 according to Margo and Goldin (1992). Second, the large change in middle class and working class might also reflect different occupational definitions for 1940 than 1950. Other years, income adjusted based on interpolation of family income distribution. For example, 1950 middle class 31.1 percent implies the highest quintile (20 percent) plus 11.1/20 of the next highest quintile.

Source: U.S. Dept of Commerce, Bureau of the Census (1951,pp. 183-185; 1967,p. 230; 1977,p. 443; 1991,pp. 392-94, 450).

Using the 1991 Consumer Expenditure Survey's derived expenditures, I find that expenditures on domestic service were .067 percent for working class and .231 for all urban earners (U.S. Dept. of Labor, Bureau of Labor Statistics 1992:4-5). By algebra then (.067 x .302) + (Middle/upper exp. x .698) = .231, meaning that the middle/upper class spends .301 percent of income on domestic service – 4.5 times greater per $100 of expenditure than the working class. Applying the same methodology to appliance expenditures, the algebraic equation is (.343 x .302) + (middle/upper exp. x .698) = .311. The middle/upper expenditures on appliances is .297 percent, approximately 87 percent of working class expenditures. In comparing the same data with 1984, the domestic service pattern held up, but the appliance expenditure did not as middle class household outspent working class households (U.S. Dept. of Labor, Bureau of Labor Statistics 1985).

With these results in mind, I examined the 1972-73 data which provided more income categories, but lacked a distinct domestic service component. I applied two 'massage' techniques to the domestic service data to generate an estimate of expenditures on domestic service. Both are displayed in Table A.2. The first technique went back to the NIPA data to determine the average ratio of domestic service expenditures to personal consumption expenditures. This figure for 1972-73 was $0.54 per $100 (Lebergott 1993). Hence, the consumer expenditure survey category overstated this figure by $1.13 (see all families in Table A.2). In the first procedure I subtracted this expenditure rate from all income classes, assuming that income elasticity was one for this unknown residual added to domestic service.

The second method assumed that all households spent the same amount on the residual category – the $90 spent by the median income group. In this case, the income elasticity is zero for incomes above the median.

Since the first method may be somewhat more accurate for working class households, while the second method more accurate for middle class households, a specially weighted ratio was also determined. That ratio indicates that middle class households spent 8.2 times what working class households spent on domestic service – nearly double my prior estimate.

Given these different results from the 1991 and the 1972-73 estimations, I took an average and rounded down to the nearest whole number as a conservative estimate of the factor by which middle class households outspent working class households on domestic service. I consider this result an accurate minimal estimate of the difference between classes.

The 4.5 factor by which the middle class outspent the working class from 1991 likely overstates class differences because I used percent of income in each class, rather than percent of spending by each class. Since wealthier households save considerably more than median and lower income households, the actual number is likely higher, as demonstrated by the results of Table A.2. Had I generated the domestic service expenditures on the basis of total income, the domestic service expenditures in Table A.2 would have dropped by at least 40 percent for those above three times median income. In the estimates for table 4.9, I continue to use the income weights which downwardly biases my results in terms of what the middle class spent. Hence, one should read the domestic service expenditures as the most the working class could have possibly spent and the least the middle class could have possibly spent.

Table A.2
Estimated expenditures on domestic service by income class, 1972-73

Expenditures per $100 of Consumption

Income	(1) Domestic Service + '?'	(2) Dom. Ser. if '?'=$1.13 per $100	(3) Dom. Ser. if '?'= $90 Fixed	(4) Dom.Ser. if avg. of (2) & (3)
All families	$1.67			
Median x 0.5	1.27	$0.14	$0.00	$0.07
Median x 0.75	1.53	0.40	0.07	0.23
Median	1.13	0.00	0.00	0.00
Median x 2	1.46	0.33	0.75	0.54
Median x 3	2.21	1.08	1.67	1.38
Median x 5+	4.05	2.92	3.65	3.29
Working Class	1.32	0.19	0.03	0.11
Middle Class	1.94	0.81	1.32	1.06
Middle÷Working	1.47	4.26	37.67	9.26 8.21*

Median income range: $10,000-11,999.

Working class estimated at just over 60 percent and based on the data – not all reported above –, an even weighting of results for 0.5, 0.75 and 1.0 times median provided a fairly accurate average.

Middle class average determined by weighting the numbers in the chart starting at 'median x 2' at weights of 4, 2, 1 and 1, respectively.

* Middle class average taken by once column 2 and twice column 3 divided by Working class average taken by twice column 2 and once column 3.

Sources: U.S. Dept. of Labor, Bureau of Labor Statistics (1978, pp.:1-12), Table A.1.

Appliance expenditures for 1972-73 generally indicate that the working class spent twenty percent more than the middle class. Since 1972-73 was after the period when working class households were acquiring these appliances for the first-time (see Table 4.6), I used the slightly higher figure of 1.28 instead of 1.20 in my calculations. The equations are listed below:

Equations (exp. = expenditures):

1940 domestic: $(.573 \times .167$ exp. of middle$) + (.427 \times$ exp. of middle$) = 2.76$, which implies exp. of middle $= 5.28$ and working class exp. $= .167 \times 5.28 = 0.88$.

1940 appliances: $(.573 \times 1.28 \times$ exp. of middle$) + (.427 \times$ exp. of middle$) = 0.90$, which implies exp. of middle and working classes $= .78$ and $.99$, respectively.

1950 domestics: $(.443 \times .167$ exp. of middle$) + (.557 \times$ exp. of middle$) = 1.47$, which implies middle class $= 2.33$ and working class exp. $= 0.39$.

1950 appliances: $(.443 \times 1.28$ exp. of exp. of middle$) + (.557 \times$ exp. of middle$) = 1.61$; so middle class exp. $= 1.43$ and working class exp. $= 1.83$.

1965 domestics: $(.415 \times .167$ exp. of middle$) + (.585 \times$ exp. of middle$) = 0.78$; so middle class exp. $= 1.19$ and working class exp. $= 0.20$.

1965 appliances: $(.415 \times 1.28$ exp. of middle$) + (.585 \times$ exp. of middle$) = 1.74$; so middle class exp. $= 1.56$ and working class exp. $= 2.00$.

Bibliography

Amariglio, Jack and Callari, Antonio (1989), 'Marxian Value Theory and the Problem of the Subject: The Role of Commodity Fetishism', *Rethinking Marxism*, Vol. 2, No. 3, pp. 31-60.

Amott, Teresa and Matthaei, Julie (1996), *Race, Gender, and Work: A Multicultural Economic History of Women in the United States*, South End Press: Boston.

Barfield, Owen (1954), *History in English Words,* new edition, Faber and Faber: London.

Barrett, Michele and McIntosh, Mary (1979), 'The 'Family Wage': Some Problems for Socialists and Feminists', *Capital and Class*, Vol. 11, Summer, pp.51-72.

Bartlett, Robin and Poulton-Callahan, Charles (1982), 'Changing Family Structure and the Income Distribution of Family Income: 1951-1976', *Social Science Quarterly*, Vol. 63, No. 1, pp. 28-38.

Becker, Gary (1991), *Treatise on the Family*, revised edition, Harvard University Press: Cambridge.

Beechery, Veronica (1978), 'Women and Production: A Critical Analysis of Some Sociological Theories', in Kuhn, Annette and Wolpe, Ann Marie (eds), *Feminism and Materialism: Women and Modes of Production*, Routlege and Kegan Paul: London, pp. 155-97.

Belk, Russell W. (1988), 'Possessions and the Extended Self', *Journal of Consumer Research*, Vol. 15, September, pp. 139-68.

Bellante, Don and Foster, Ann C. (1984), 'Working Wives and Expenditure on Services', *Journal of Consumer Research*, Vol. 11, September, pp. 700-707.

Benson, Barbara (1947), 'Do Men or Women Lead the Harder Life?', *Ladies' Home Journal,* May, pp. 44-45,152.

Benson, Susan Porter (1986), *Countercultures: Saleswomen, Managers, and Customers in American Department Stores, 1890-1940,* University of Illinois Press: Urbana.

Berger, Peter L., Berger, Brigitte, and Kellner, Hansfield (1974), *The Homeless Mind,* Random House: New York.

Berk, Sarah Fenstermaker.(1985), *The Gender Factory: the Apportionment of Work In American Households,* Plenum Press: New York.

Birken, Lawrence (1988), *Consuming Desire: Sexual Science and the Emergence of a Culture of Abundance, 1871-1914,* Cornell University Press: Ithaca.

Blair, Anita; Ehrenreich, Barbara; Lewis; Jeanne, Hochshild; Arlie Russell; McKenna, Elizabeth Perle (1997), 'Giving Women the Business: On Winning, Losing, and Leaving te Corporate Game', *Harper's Magazine,* Vol. 295, December, pp. 47-58.

Blair, Sampson Lee and Johnson, Michael P. (1992), 'Wives' Perceptions of Fairness of the Division of Household Labor: The Intersection of Housework and Ideology', *Journal of Marriage and Family,* Vol. 54, August, pp. 570-81.

Blank, Rebecca M. (1988), 'Women's Paid Work, Household Income, Household Well-being', in Rix, Sara E. (ed.), *The American Woman 1988-1989: A Status Report,* W.W. Norton: New York.

_____ (1989), 'The Role of Part-time Work in Women's Labor Market Choices Over Time', *American Economic Review,* Vol. 79, May, pp. 295-99.

Blood, Robert O. Jr.(1963), 'Rejoinder to "Measurement and Bases of Family Power"', *Journal of Marriage and Family,* Vol. 25, pp. 475-78.

Blood, Robert O. Jr. and Wolfe, Donald M (1960), *Husbands and Wives: The Dynamics of Family Living,* Free Press: New York.

Bluestone, Barry and Harrison, Bennett (1982), *The Deindustrialization of America: Plant Closings, Community abandonment, and the Dismantling of Basic Communities,* Basic Books: New York.

Blumberg, Paul (1974), 'The Decline and Fall of the Status Symbol: Some Thoughts on Status in a Post-Industrial Society', *Social Problems,* Vol. 21, pp. 480-98.

Blumberg, Rae Lesser (1984), 'A General Theory of Gender Stratification' in Collins, Randall (ed.), *Sociological Theory,* Josey-Bass: San Francisco.

_____ (1991), 'Introduction', in Blumberg, Rae Lesser, *Gender, Family, and Economy: The Triple Overlap,* Sage: Newbury Park, pp. 7-34

Blumstein, Philip and Schwartz, Pepper (1991), 'Money and Ideology: Their Impact on Power and the Division of Household Labor', in Blumberg, Rae Leser, *Gender, Family, and Economy: The Triple Overlap*, Sage: Newbury Park, pp. 261-88

Boland, Lawrence A. (1992), *The Principles of Economics: Some Lies My Teachers Told Me*, Routledge: New York.

Bose, Christine. 1980, 'Social Status of the Homemaker', in Berk, Sarah Fenstermaker (ed.), *Women and Household Labor*, Sage: Beverly Hills.

Boserup, Ester (1987), 'Inequality Between the Sexes', in Eatwell, John, Migate, Murray, Newman, Peter (eds.), *The New Palgrave: A Dictionary of Economics*, : Macmillan: New York, pp.824-27.

Bourdieu, Pierre (1984), *Distinction: A Social Critique of the Judgement of Taste*, Nice, Richard (translator), Harvard University Press: Cambridge.

Bowen, William G. and Finegan, T. Aldich (1969), *The Economics of Labor Force Participation*, Princeton University Press: Princeton, NJ.

Bowlby, R. (1985), *Just Looking: Consumer Culture in Dreiser, Gissing and Zola*, Methuen: New York.

Brackett, Jean (1969), 'New BLS Budgets', *Monthly Labor Review*, Vol. 92, No. 4, pp. 3-16.

Brennan, Geoffrey (1990), 'Comment: What Might Rationality Fail to Do?', in Cook, Karen Scheers and Levi, Margaret (eds.), *Limits of Rationality*, Chicago University Press: Chicago.

Brenner, Reuven (1987), *Rivalry in Business, Science, Among Nations*, Cambridge University Press: Cambridge.

Broome, John (1991), 'Utility', *Journal of Economics and Philosophy*, Vol. 7, No. 1, pp. 1-12.

Brown, Clair (1985), 'An Institutional Model of Wives' Work Decisions', *Industrial Relations*, Vol. 24, No. 2, pp. 187-204.

_____ (1987), 'Consumption Norms, Work Roles, and Economic Growth, 1918-80', in Brown, Clair and Pechman, Joseph A. (eds.). *Gender in the Workplace*, Brookings: Washington, D.C.

Burtless, Gary (1990), 'Earnings Inequality over the Business and Demographic Cycles', in Burtless, Gary (ed.), *A Future of Lousy Jobs? The Changing Structure of U.S. Wages*, Brookings: Washington, D.C., pp. 77-117.

Cain, Glen G. (1966), *Married Women in the Labor Force: An Economic Analysis*, University of Chicago Press: Chicago.

Calhoun, Arthur, W. (1918), *A Social History of the American Family*, Vol. II, The Arthur H. Clark Co.: Cleveland.

Campbell, Colin (1987), *The Romantic Ethic and Spirit of Modern Consumerism*, Basil Blackwell: New York.

_____ (1993), 'The Desire for the New: Its Nature and Social Location as Presented in Theories of Fashion and Modern Consumerism', in Silverstone, Roger and Hirsch, Eric (eds.), *Consuming Technologies*, Routledge: New York.

Caplovitz, David (1964), 'The Problems of Blue-Collar Consumers', in Shostak, Arthur B. and Gomberg, William (eds.), *Blue-Collar World: Studies of the American Worker*, Prentice Hall: Englewood Cliffs, pp. 110-20.

Carson, Cary (1994), 'The Consumer Revolution in Colonial America: Why Demand?', in Carson, Cary, Hoffman, Ronald, and Albert, Peter J. (eds.), *Of Consuming Interests: The Style of Life in the Eighteenth Century*, University Press of Virginia: Charlottesville, VA.

Chandler, Alfred D. Jr (1977), *The Visible Hand: The Managerial Revolution in American Business*, Harvard University Press: Cambridge.

Chapin, Robert Coit (1909), *The Standard of Living among Workingmen's Families in New York City*, Russell Sage Found, Charities Publication Committee: New York.

Chase, Stuart (1926), 'Wasting Women', *The Survey*, Vol. 57, No. 5, pp. 268-70.

Chinoy, Eli (1952), 'Aspirations of Automobile Workers', *American Journal of Sociology*, Vol. 57, pp. 453-59.

Chodorow, Nancy (1978), *Mothering: Psychoanalysis and the Social Organization of Gender*, University of California Press: Berkeley.

Clower, Robert W. (1952), 'Professor Duesenberry and the Traditional Theory', *Review of Economic Studies*, Vol. 19, No. 3, pp. 165-78.

Coleman, Marion Tolbert (1991), 'The Division of Household Labor: Suggestions for Future Empirical Consideration', in Blumberg, Rae Lesser (ed.), *Gender, Family, and Economy: The Triple Overlap*, Russel Sage: Newbury Park, pp. 245-60.

Collins, Randall (1991), 'Women and Men in the Class Structure', in Blumberg, Rae Lesser (ed.), *Gender, Family, and Economy: The Triple Overlap*, Russel Sage: Newbury Park, pp. 52-73.

Connell, R. (1987), *Gender and Power: Society, the Person and Sexual Politics*, Stanford University Press: Stanford.

Coverman, Shelley (1985), 'Explaining Husbands' Participation in Domestic Labor', *The Sociological Quarterly*, Vol. 26, No. 1, pp. 81-97.

Coulson, Mugas, and Wainwright (1975), 'The Housewife and Her Labour Under Capitalism: A Critique', *New Left Review*, Vol. 89, pp. 59-71.

Cowan, Ruth Schwartz (1983), *More Work for Mother: The Ironies of Household Technology from the Open Hearth to the Microwave*, Basic Books: New York.

Cross, Gary (1993), *Time and Money: The Making of Consumer Culture*, Routledge: New York.

Davis, Ethelyn (1964), 'Careers as Concerns of Blue Collar Girls', in Shostak, Arthur B. and Gomberg, William, *Blue-Collar World: Studies of the American Worker*, Prentice Hall: Englewood Cliffs, NJ, pp. 154-64.

DeScheweintz, Karl (1928), 'Are the Poor Really Poor?', *The Survey*, Vol. 59, No. 8, pp. 517-19.

Diderot, Denis (1964), 'Regrets on Parting with my Old Dressing Gown', in Barzun, Jacques and Bowen, Ralph H. (translators), *Rameau's Nephew and other Works by Denis Diderot*, Bobbs-Merrill: New York, pp. 309-17.

DiMaggio, Paul (1990), 'Cultural Aspects of Economic Action and Organization', in Friedland, Roger and Robertson, Friedland (eds.), *Beyond the Marketplace: Rethinking Economy and Society*, Aldine de Gruyter: New York.

Dooley, Martin D. and Gottschalk, Peter (1982), 'Does A Younger Male Labor Force Mean Greater Earnings Inequality', *Monthly Labor Review*, Vol. 105, No. 11, pp. 42-45.

_____ (1984), 'Earnings Inequality Among Males in the United States: Trends and Effects of Labor Force Growth', *Journal of Political Economy*, Vol. 92, February, pp. 58-89.

Douglas, Ann (1977), *The Feminization of American Culture*, Alfred A. Knopf: New York.

Douglas, Mary and Isherwood, Baron (1979), *The World of Goods*, Basic Books: New York.

Douglas, Paul H (1966 [1930]), *Real Wages in the United States: 1890-1926*, Augustus Kelley: New York.

Duesenberry, James S. (1949), *Income, Saving and the Theory of Consumer Behavior*, Harvard University Press: Cambridge.

Durand, John (1968 [1948]), *The Labor Force in the United States, 1890-1960*, Social Science Research Council: New York.

Durkheim, Emile (1984 [1893]), *The Division of Labor in Society*, Free Press: New York.

Easterlin, Richard A. (1968), *Population, Labor Force, and Long Swings in Economic Growth*, National Bureau of Economic Research: New York.

Ehrenreich, Barbara and English, Deidre (1979) *For Her Own Good: 150 Years of the Expert's Advice to Women*, Anchor Press: New York.

Eisenstein, Zillah R. (1979), 'Developing a Theory of Capitalist Patriarchy and Socialist Feminism', in Eisenstein, Zillah (ed.), *Capitalist Patriarchy and the Case for Socialist Feminism*, Monthly Review Press: New York, pp. 5-40.

Elliott, John E. (1981), *Marx and Engels on Economics, Politics, and Society*, Goodyear: Santa Monica.

Engels, Frederick (1891), *The Origin of the Family, Private Property and the State*, 4th edition, International Publishers: Moscow.

England, Paula (1993), 'The Separate Self: Androcentric Bias in Neoclassical Assumptions', in Ferber, Marianne A. and Nelson, Julie A. (eds.), *Beyond Economic Man: Feminist Theory and Economics*, Chicago University Press: Chicago, pp. 37-53.

_____ (1989), 'A Feminist Critique of Rational-Choice Theories: Implications for Sociology', *American Sociologist*, Vol. 20, pp. 14-28.

England, Paula and Farkas, George (1986), *Households, Employment, and Gender: A Social, Economic, and Demographic View*, Aldine de Gruyer: Hawthorne, NY.

Ferree, Myra Marx (1990), 'Beyond Separate Spheres: Feminism and Family Research', *Journal of Marriage and Family*, Vol. 52, November, pp. 866-84.

Fine, Ben (1992), *Women's Employment and the Capitalist Family*, Routledge: New York.

Folbre, Nancy and Abel, Marjorie (1989), 'Women's Work and Women's Households: Gender Bias in the U.S. Census', *Social Forces*, Vol. 56, No. 3, pp. 545-76.

Fox, Bonnie (1980), 'Women's Productive Role in the Household and Wage Work Force in the Twentieth Century', doctoral dissertation, University of Alberta: Alberta, British Columbia.

Fraad, Harriet, Resnick, Stephen, and Wolff, Richard (1989), 'For Every Knight in Shining Armor, There's a Castle Waiting to be Cleaned: A Marxist-Feminist Analysis of the Household', *Rethinking Marxism*, Vol. 2, No. 4, pp. 11-69.

Friedman, Milton (1962), *Price Theory*, Aldene: Chicago.

Gardiner, Jean (1975), 'Women's Domestic Labour', *New Left Review*, Vol. 89, pp. 47-58.

Geib-Gunderson, Lisa (1995), 'The Undercount of Productive Women in the U.S., 1880-1910', paper presented at annual Western Economic Association meetings, San Diego, CA, May.

Gerson, Kathleen (1985), *Hard Choices: How Women Decide about Work, Career, and Motherhood*, University of California Press: Berkeley.

Giedion, Siegfried (1948), *Mechanization Takes Command*, Oxford University Press: New York.

Gilman, Charlotte Perkins (1913), 'The Waste of Private Housekeeping', *The Annals of the American Academy of Political and Social Science*, Vol. 18, July, pp. 91-95.

_____ (1966), *Women and Economics*, Harper & Row: New York.

Gintis, Herbert and Bowles, Samuel (1981), 'Structure and Practice in the Labor Theory of Value', *Review of Radical Political Economics*, Vol. 12, No. 4, pp. 1-26.

Glasberg, Ronald (1985), 'Sam and His Laugh: A Comic Strip Reflection of Turn of the Century America', *Journal of American Culture*, Vol. 8, No. 1, pp. 87-94.

Goffman, Erving (1959), *The Presentation of Self in Everyday Life*, Doubleday: New York.

Goldin, Claudia (1979), 'Household and Market Production of Families in a Late Nineteenth Century City', *Explorations in Economic History*, Vol. 16, April, p. 111-31.

_____ (1990), *Understanding the Gender Gap: An Economic History of American Women*, Oxford University Press: New York.

Goldin, Claudia and Margo, Robert A. (1992), 'The Great Compression: The Wage Structure in the United States at Mid-Century' *Quarterly Journal of Economics*, Vol. 57, No. 1, pp. 4-34.

Gordon, Jean and McArthur, Jan (1985), 'American Women and Domestic Consumption, 1800-1925: Four Interpretive Themes', *Journal of American Culture*, Vol. 18, No. 3, pp. 35-46.

Gorz, Andre (1989), *Critique of Economic Reason*, in Handerside, Gillian and Turner, Chris (translators), Verso: New York.

Gramsci, Antonio (1971), *Selections from the Prison Notebooks*, in Hoare, Quintin and Smith, Geoffrey Nowell (eds. and trans.), International Publishers: New York.

Greenstein, Theodore N. (1990), 'Marital Disruption and the Employment of Married Women', *Journal of Marriage and Family*, Vol. 52, August, pp. 657-76.

Groom, Phyllis (1967), 'A New City Worker's Family Budget', *Monthly Labor Review*, Vol. 90, No. 11, pp. 1-5.

Hallidy, Evelyn G. and Noble, Isabel (1930), 'Hows and Whys of Making Muffins', *Ladies' Home Journal*, Vol. 47, July, pp. 84, 97.

Hanson, Sandra L. and Ooms, Theodora (1991), 'The Economic Costs and Rewards of Two-Earner, Two-Parent Families', *Journal of Marriage and Family*, Vol. 53, August, pp. 622-34.

Harrison, John (1973), 'The Political Economy of Housework', *Bulletin of the Conference of Socialist Economists*, Vol. Winter, pp. 35-52.

Hart, James (1950), *The Popular Book: A History of America's Literary Taste*, University of California Press: Berkeley.

Hartmann, Heidi (1974), 'Capitalism and Women's Work in the Home, 1900-1930', doctoral dissertation, Yale University: New Haven.

_____ (1979), 'Capitalism, Patriarchy and Job Segregation by Sex', in *Capitalist Patriarchy and the Case for Socialist Feminism*, Eisenstein, Zillah (ed.), Monthly Review Press: New York, pp. 206-47.

_____ (1981), 'The Family as the Locus of Gender, Class and Political Struggle', *Signs*, Vol. 6, No. 3, pp. 366-94.

Hays, Constance L. (1998), 'First Lessons in the Power of Money', *New York Times*, April 12.

Heath, Aloise Buckley (1947), 'A Housewife Looks at Soap Opera', *Ladies' Home Journal*, Vol. April, pp. 23,246,249.

Heer, David (1963), 'Dominance and the Working Wife', in *The Employed Mother in America*, in Nye, F. Ivan and Hoffman, Lois Waldis (eds.), Rand McNally: Chicago, pp. 251-62.

Henderson, Yandell and Davis, Maurice R. (eds.) (1928), *Income and Living Costs of University Faculty*, Yale University Press: New Haven.

Henle, Peter and Ryscavage, Paul (1980), 'The Distribution of Earned Income among Men and Women, 1958-1977', *Monthly Labor Review*, Vol. 103, No. 4, pp. 3-10.

Hirsch, Fred (1977), *Social Limits to Growth*, Harvard University Press: Cambridge.

Hoffman, Lois Waldis (1963), 'Parental Power Relations and the Division of Household Tasks', in *The Employed Mother in America*, Nye, F. Ivan and Hoffman, Lois Waldis (eds.), Rand McNally: Chicago, pp. 231-40.

Hoffman, Ronald (1994), 'Preface', in Carson, Cary, Hoffman, Ronald, and Albert, Peter J. (eds.), *Of Consuming Interests: The Style of Life in the Eighteenth Century*, University Press of Virginia: Charlottesville.

Hornung, Carlton A, McCullough, B.C., and Sugimoto, Taichi (1981), 'Status Relationships in Marriage: Risk Factors in Spouse Abuse', *Journal of Marriage and Family*, Vol. 43, pp. 349-59.

Howell, David R. (1995), 'Collapsing Wages and Rising Inequality: Has Computerization Shifted the Demand for Skills?', *Challenge*, Vol. 27, January-February, pp. 27-35.

Huber, Joan (1991), 'A Theory of Family, Economy, and Gender', in *Gender, Family, and Economy: The Triple Overlap*, Blumberg, Rae Lesser (ed.), Russell Sage: Newbury Park, pp. 35-51.

Hughes, Everett C. (1945), 'Dilemmas and Contradictions of Status', *American Journal of Sociology*, Vol. 50, pp. 353-59.

Hughes, Gwendolyn Berry (1929), 'Mothers in Industry', *Annals of the American Academy of Political and Social Science*' Vol. 34, pp. 315-24.

Humphries, Jane (1977), 'Class Struggle and the Persistence of the Working-Class Family', *Cambridge Journal of Economics*, Vol. 1, Sept., pp. 241-58.

_____ (1993), 'The Sexual Division of Labor and Social Control: An Interpretation', *Review of Radical Political Economics*, Vol. 23, Nos. 3&4, pp. 269-96.

Humphries, Jane and Rubery, Jill (1984), 'The Reconstruction of the Supply-side of the Labour Market: The Relative Automony of Social Reproduction', *Cambridge Journal of Economics*, Vol. 8, Dec., pp. 331-46.

Iglehart, Alfreda P. (1979), *Married Women and Work: 1957 and 1976*, Lexington Books: Lexington.

Jenson, Joan M. (1980), 'Cloth, Butter and Boarders: Women's Household Production for the Market', *Review of Radical Political Economics*, Vol. 12, No. 2, pp. 14-24.

Jevons, Wilfred S. (1871), *The Theory of Political Economy*, MacMillan: London.

Katz, Lawrence F. and Murphy, Kevin M. (1992), 'Changes in Relative Wages, 1963-1987: Supply and Demand Factors', *Quarterly Journal of Economics*, Vol. 57, No. 1, pp. 35-78.

Kellogg, Lester and Dorothy Brady, Dorothy (1948), 'The City Worker's Family Budget', *Monthly Labor Review.*, Vol. 71, No. 1, pp. 133-70.

Kessler-Harris, Alice (1982), *Out to Work: A History of Wage-earning Women in the United States*, Oxford University Press: New York.

Knapp, Eunice (1951), 'Family Budget of City Worker', *Monthly Labor Review*, Vol. 74, No. 2, pp. 149-55.

_____ (1952), 'City Worker's Family Budget for October', *Monthly Labor Review*, Vol. 75, No. 4, pp. 520-24.

Kneeland, Hildegarde (1929), 'Is the Modern Housewife a Lady of Leisure?', *The Survey*, Vol. 60, No.5, pp.301-302,333,336.

Komarovsky, Mirra (1962), *Blue Collar Marriage*, Random House: New York.

Komter, Aafe (1989), 'Hidden Power in Marriage', *Gender & Society*, Vol. 3, No. 2, pp. 187-216.

Kurtz, Demie (1995), *For Richer, For Poorer: Mothers Confront Divorce*, Routledge: New York.

Kyrk, Hazel (1923), *A Theory of Consumption*, Houghton Mifflin: Boston.

_____ (1933), *Economic Problems of the Family*, Harper & Brothers: New York.

Laerman, Rudi (1993), 'Learning to Consume: Early Department Stores and the Shaping of the Modern Consumer Culture (1860-1910)', *Theory, Culture & Society*, Vol. 10, pp. 79-102.

Lamale, Helen H. and Stotz, Margaret S. (1960), 'The Interim City Worker's Family Budget', *Monthly Labor Review*, Vol. 83, No. 8, pp. 785-805.

Lancaster, Kelvin (1971), *Consumer Demand: A New Approach*, Columbia University Press: New York.

Lane, Robert E. (1991), *The Market Experience*, Cambridge University Press: Cambridge.

_____ (1994), 'The Road Not Taken: Friendship, Consumerism, and Happiness', *Critical Review*, Vol. 8, No. 4, pp. 521-554.

Leach, William (1984), 'Transformations in a Culture of Consumption: Women and Department Stores, 1890-1925', *Journal of American History*, Vol. 71, No. 2, pp. 319-42.

_____ (1993), *Land of Desire: Merchant Power and the Rise of a New American Culture*, Pantheon: New York.

Lears, T. J. Jackson (1983), 'From Salvation to Self-Realization: Advertising and the Therapeutic Roots of the Consumer Culture 1880-1930', in Fox, Richard Wrightman and Lears, T. J. Jackson, *The Culture of Consumption: Critical Essays in American History,* Pantheon: New York, pp. 1-38.

Lebergott, Stanley (1976), *The American Economy: Income, Wealth, and Want*, Princeton University Press: Princeton.

_____ (1987), 'Comments on Clair Brown's "Consumption Norms, Work Roles, and Economic Growth, 1918-80"', in Brown, Clair and Pechman, Joseph A. (eds.), *Gender in the Workplace*, Brookings: Washington, D.C.

_____ (1993), *Pursuing Happiness: American Consumers in the Twentieth Century*, Princeton University Press: Princeton.

Lebowitz, Michael A. (1982), "The One-Sidedness of 'Capital'", *Review of Radical Political Economics*, Vol. 14, No. 4, pp. 42-51.

_____ (1991), 'The Significance of Marx's Missing Book on Wage-Labor', *Rethinking Marxism*, Vol. 4, No. 2, pp. 105-18.

Leibenstein, Harvey (1950), 'Bandwagon, Snob and Veblen Effects', *Quarterly Journal of Economics*, May.

Leiss, William (1983), 'The Icons of the Marketplace', *Theory, Culture & Society*, Vol. 1, No. 3.

Leon, Carol and Bednarzik, Robert W. (1978), 'A Profile of Women on Part-time Schedules', *Monthly Labor Review*, Vol. 101, No. 10, pp. 3-12.

Leven, Maurice, Moulton, Harold G., and Wharburton, Clark (1934), *America's Capacity to Consume*, Brookings: Washington, D.C.

Levine, David (1988), *Needs, Rights, and the Market*, Lynne-Rienner: Boulder.

_____ (1989), 'The Sense of Theory in Political Economy', *Rethinking Marxism*, Vol. 2, No. 1, pp. 29-49.

The Literature of Business (1905), *The Nation*, November 15, pp. 409-410.

Love, Belle (1930), 'Plain Cake', *Ladies' Home Journal*, Vol. 47, September, p. 94.

Lundberg, Shelly and Pollak, Robert A. (1993), 'Separate Spheres: Bargaining and the Marriage Market', *Journal of Political Economy*, Vol. 100, No. 6, pp. 988-1010.

_____ (1994), 'Noncooperative Bargaining Models of Marriage', *American Economic Review*, Vol. 84, No. 2, pp. 132-37.

Lynd, Robert S. and Lynd, Helen Merrell (1929), *Middletown: A Study in American Culture*, Harcourt Brace and Co.: New York.

Manser, Marilyn and Brown, Murray (1980), 'Marriage and Household Decision-Making: A Bargaining Analysis', *International Economic Review*, Vol. 21, No. 1, pp. 31-44.

Marglin, Stephen A. (1974), 'What Do Bosses Do? The Origins and Functions of Hierarchy in Capitalist Production', *Review of Radical Political Economics*, Vol. 6, pp. 33-60.

Marx, Karl (1964), *The Economic and Philosphical Manuscripts of 1844*, International Publishers: New York.

_____ (1967 [1867]), *Capital*, Vol. 1, International Publishers: New York.

Marx, Karl and Frederick Engels, (1954 [1948]), *The Communist Manifesto*, Gateway Press: Chicago.

_____ (1986), *The German Ideology*, International Publishers: New York.

Mason, Karen Oppenheim; Czajka, John L.; and Arber, Sara (1976), 'Change in U.S. Women's Sex-Role Attitudes, 1964-1974', *American Sociological Review*, Vol. 41, No. 4, pp. 573-596.

Matthaei, Julie A. (1982), *An Economic History of Women in American: Women's Work, the Sexual Division of Labor, and the Development of Capitalism*, Scocken Books: New York.

Matthews, Glenna (1987), *Just a Housewife: The Rise and Fall of Domesticity in America*, Oxford University Press: New York.

May, Martha (1982), 'The Historical Problem of the Family Wage: The Ford Motor Company and the Five Dollar Day', *Feminist Studies*, Volume 8, No. 2, pp. 399-424.

McCracken, Grant (1988), *Culture and Consumption: New Approaches to the Symbolic Character of Consumer Good and Activities*, Indiana University Press: Bloomington.

McCraw, Louise (1977), 'Family Budget's Cost Continued to Climb in 1976', *Monthly Labor Review*, Vol. 100, No. 7, pp. 35-39.

McDonald, Gerald W. (1980), 'Family Power: The Assessment of a Decade of Theory and Research, 1970-79', *Journal of Marriage and Family*, Vol. 42, No. 2, pp. 841-851.

McElroy, Marjorie B. and Horney, Mary J. (1981), 'Nash-Bargained Household Decisions: Toward a Generalization of the Theory of Demand', *International Economic Review*, Vol. 22, No. 2, pp. 333-49.

McHale, Susan M. and Crouter, Ann (1992), 'You Can't Always Get What You Want: Incongruence Between Sex-Role Attitudes and Family Work Roles and Its Implications for Marriage', *Journal of Marriage and Family*, Vol. 54, August, pp. 537-47.

McKendrick, Neil, Brewer, John, and Plumb, J. H. (1982), *The Birth of a Consumer Society: The Commercialization of Eighteenth-Century England*, Indiana University Press: Bloomington.

McMahon, John R. (1920), 'Making Housekeeping Automatic: The Bride Was Promised "Many Servants" But They Were Not Visible', *Ladies' Home Journal*, September, pp. 3-4, 205.

McNally, Mary (1980), 'Consumption, Utility and Social Process', *Journal of Post Keynesian Economics*, Vol. 2, No. 3, pp. 381-390.

Meeker, Royal (1919), 'What is the American Standard of Living?', *Monthly Labor Review*, Vol. 9, No. 1, pp. 1-13.

Menger, Carl (1976 [1871]), *Principles of Economics*, New York University Press: New York.

Merton, Robert K. (1968), *Social Theory and Social Structure*, Revised and Enlarged edition, Free Press: Glencoe, IL

Mincer, Jacob (1962), 'Labor Force Participation of Married Women', in Lewis, Greg (ed.), *Aspects of Labor Economics*, Universities National Conference Bureau Conference Series No. 14, Arno Press: Princeton.

Mishel, Lawrence and Frankel, David M. (1991), *State of Working America: 1990-91 Edition*, Economic Policy Institute, M.E. Sharpe: New York.

Mitchell, John L. (1992), 'Baggin' and Saggin'': Parents Wary of a Big Fashion Trend', *Los Angeles Times*, Sept. 28, Metro Section, p. 1.

Mitchell, S. Weir (1877), *Fat and Blood and How to Marry Them*, Lippencott: Philadelphia.

Modell, John and Hareven, Tamara K. Hareven (1973), 'Urbanization and the Malleable Household: An Examination of Boarding and Lodging in American Families', *Journal of Marriage and Family*, Vol. 35, No. 3, pp. 467-479.

Moen, Carol (1985), 'Continutities and Discontinuities in Women's Labor Force Activity', in Elder, Glen H. (ed.) *Life Course Dynamics: Trajectories and Transitions, 1968-1980*, Cornell University Press: Ithaca.

Moore, Kristin A. and Hofferth, Sandra L. (1979), 'Women and Their Children', in Smith, Ralph E. (ed.), *The Subtle Revolution: Women at Work*, Urban Institute: Washington, D.C., pp. 125-58.

Morgan, James; David, Martin H.; Cohen, Wilber J., and Brazer, Harvey E. (1962), *Income and Welfare in the United States*. McGraw-Hill: New York.

Morgan, James; Sirageldin, Ismail; and Baerwaldt, Nancy (1966), *Productive Americans: A Study of How Individuals Contribute to Economic Growth*, Institute for Social Research: Ann Arbor.

Myrdall, Alva and Klein, Viola (1968 [1956]), *Women's Two Roles: Home and Work*, Routledge and Kegan Paul: London.

Nesbitt, Florence (1919), *The Chicago Standard Budget for Dependent Families*, Committee on Relief of Chicago County of Social Agencies: Chicago.

Nienberg, B.M. (1923), *The Woman Home-Maker in the City*, Bureau of the Census, Government Printing Office: Washington, D.C.

Olney, Martha (1991), *Buy Now, Pay Later: Advertising, Credit, and Consumer Durables in the 1920s*, University of North Carolina Press: Chapel Hill.

Olsen, Randall J. (1994), 'Fertility and the Size of the U.S. Labor Force', *Journal of Economic Literature*, Vol. 32, No. 1, pp. 60-100.

Oppenheimer, Valerie Kincade (1970), *The Female Labor Force in the United States: Demographic and Economic Factors Governing Its Growth and Changing Composition*, University of California Population Monograph Series, No. 5.: Berkeley.

_____ (1977), 'Sociology of Women's Economic Role in the Family', *American Sociological Review*, Vol. 42, pp. 387-406.

Owen, J.D. (1971), 'The Demand for Leisure', *Journal of Political Economy*, Vol. 74, January, pp. 56-76.

Palmer, Phyllis (1989), *Domesticity and Dirt: Housewives and Domestic Servants in the United States, 1920-1945*, Temple University Press: Philadelphia.

Parsons, Talcott (1954), *Essays in Sociological Theory*, Free Press: New York.

Parsons, Talcott and Bales, Robert F. (1956), *Family: Socialization and Interaction Process*, Routledge & Kegan Paul: London.

Peixotto, Jessica B. (1927), *Getting and Spending at the Professional Standard of Living*, Macmillan: New York.

Perrett, Antoinette (1923), 'Attached Garages: The Garage Becomes Part of the House', *Ladies' Home Journal*, March, p. 48.

Pleck, Joseph (1985), *Working Wives/Working Husbands*, Sage: Beverly Hills, CA.

Pollak, Robert A. (1970), 'Habit Formation and Dynamic Demand Functions', *Journal of Political Economy*, Vol. 78, No. 4, pp. 745-63.

Popenoe, David (1993), 'American Family Decline, 1960-1990: A Review and Appraisal', *Journal of Marriage and Family*, Vol. 55, August, pp. 527-555.

Power, Marilyn (1983), 'From Home Production to Wage Labor: Women as a Reserve Army of Labor', *Review of Radical Political Economics*, Vol. 15, No. 1, pp. 71-91.

Pruette, Lorine (1929), 'The Married Woman and the Part-Time Job', *Annals of the American Academy of Social and Political Science*, Vol. 34, pp. 301-14.

Pyke, Karen D. (1994), 'Women's Employment as a Gift or a Burden? Marital Power Across Marriage, Divorce, and Remarriage', *Gender & Society*, Vol. 8, No. 1, pp. 73-91.

Rainwater, Lee, Coleman, Richard P. Coleman, and Handel, Gerald (1959), *Workingman's Wife: Her Personality, World and Life Style*, Oceana Publications: New York.

Rainwater, Lee. (1974), *What Money Buys*, Basic Books: New York.

Richardson, J.E. (1933), *The Use of Time by Rural Homemakers in Montana*, Montana Agricultural Experimentation Bulletin 271, Montana State College: Bozeman.

Robinson, Joan (1962), *Economic Philosophy*, Doubleday: New York.

Robinson, John P. (1980), 'Household Technology and Household Work', in Berk, Sarah Fenstermaker (ed.), *Women and Household Labor*, Sage: Beverly Hills.

Rose, Gillian (1978), *The Melancholy Science: An Introduction to the Thought of Theodor W. Adorno*, MacMillan: London.

Rosenzweig, Roy (1983), *Eight Hours for What We Will: Workers and Leisure in an Industrial City, 1870-1920*, Cambridge University Press: New York.

Royal, Beatrice Baxter (1923), 'Colonial Trays That You Can Paint', *Ladies' Home Journal*, March, p. 62.

Rubin, Rose M. and Riney, Bobye J. (1995), *Working Wives and Dual-Earner Families*, Praeger: Westport, CT.

Ryscavage, Paul (1970), 'More Wives in the Labor Force Have Husbands with "Above-average" Incomes', *Monthly Labor Review*, June, pp. 40-42.

Sacks, Karen (1974), 'Engels Revisited: Women, the Organization of Production, and Private Property', in Rosaldo, Michelle Zimbalist and Lamphere, Louise (eds.), *Woman, Culture, and Society,* Stanford University Press: Stanford, pp.207-22.

Sahlins, Marshall (1972), *Stone Age Economics*, Aldine Atherton: Chicago.

Sassoon, Anne Showstack (1987), 'Introduction: the personal and the intellectual, fragments and order, international trends and national specificities', in Sassoon, Anne Showstack, *Women and the State: The Shifting Boundaries of Public and Private*, Hutchinson: London.

Schor, Juliet (1991), *The Overworked American: The Unexpected Decline of Leisure*, New York: Basic Books.

Schultz, T. Paul (1990), 'Testing the Neoclassical Model of Family Labor Supply and Fertility', *Journal of Human Resources*, Vol. 25, No. 4, pp. 599-634.

Sears Catalog no. 117. (1969 [1908]), Schroeder, Jr. , Joseph J. (ed.), Follett Publication Co.: Chicago.

Seccombe, Wally (1974), 'The Housewife and Her Labour under Capitalism', *New Left Review*, Vol. 83, pp. 3-24.

_____ (1980), 'Domestic Labour and the Working-class Household', in Fox, Bonnie (ed.), *Hidden in the Household: Women's Domestic Labour Under Capitalism*, The Women's Press: Toronto.

Seo, Diane (1993), 'Urban Fashion's Big Attraction: For Many Students, Brand-Name Clothes and Shoes Are the Ticket to Status. But Being Trendy Costs a Lot of Money – and It Can Be Dangerous, Too', *Los Angeles Times* Nov. 21, City Times Section, p. 17.

Seiz, Janet (1991), 'The Bargaining Approach and Feminist Methodology', *Review of Radical Political Economics*, Vol. 23, No. 1&2, pp. 22-29.

Sen, Gita (1980), 'The Sexual Division of Labor and the Working Class Family: Towards a Conceptual Synthesis of Class Relations and the Subordination of Women', *Review of Radical Political Economics*, Vol. 12, No. 2, pp. 76-86.

Sennett, Richard and Cobb, Jonathon (1973), *The Hidden Injuries of Class*, Random House: New York.

Sexton, Patricia Cayo (1964), 'Wife of the "Happy Worker"', in Shostak, Arthur B. and Gomberg, William (eds.), *Blue-Collar World: Studies of the American Worker*, Prentice-Hall: Englewood Cliffs, NJ.

Shaw, William Howard (1947),. *Value of Commodity Output Since 1869*, No. 48. National Bureau of Economic Research: New York.

Smuts, Robert (1960), 'The Female Labor Force: A Case Study in the Interpretation of Historical Statistics', *Journal of the American Statistical Association*, Vol. 55, March, pp. 71-79.

Sobol, Marion G. (1963), 'Commitment to Work', in Nye, F. Ivan and Hoffman, Lois Waldis (eds.), *The Employed Mother in America*, Rand McNally: Chicago, pp. 40-63.

Stafford, Frank P. and Duncan, Greg J. (1985), 'The Use of Time and Technology by Households in the United States', in Juster, F. Thomas and Stafford, Frank P. (eds.), *Time, Goods, and Well-Being*, Institute for Social Research The University of Michigan: Ann Arbor.

Stephens, Jane (1985), 'Breezes of Discontent: A Historical Perspective of Anxiety Based Illness Among Women', *Journal of American Culture*, Vol. 8, No. 4, pp. 3-10.

Stigler, George J. (1946), *Domestic Servants in the United States, 1900-1940*, Occasional Paper 24, National Bureau of Economic Research: New York.

Stigler, George J. and Becker, Gary S. (1977), 'De Gustibus Non Est Disputandum', *American Economic Review*, Vol. 67, No. 2, pp. 77-90.

Stowe, Harriet Beecher (1896), *Household Papers and Stories, the Writings of Harriet Beecher Stowe*, Vol. 8, Houghton Mifflin: Boston.

Strasser, Susan (1982), *Never Done: A History of American Housework*, Pantheon: New York.

_____ (1989), *Satisfaction Guaranteed: The Making of the American Mass Market*, Pantheon: New York.

Strober, Myra. H. (1977), 'Wives' Labor Force Behavior and Family Consumption Patterns', *American Economic Review*, Vol. 67, No. 1, pp. 410-17.

Strober, Myra H. and Weinberg, Charles B. (1980), 'Strategies Used by Working and Nonworking Wives to Reduce Times Pressures', *Journal of Consumer Research*, Vol. 6, March, pp. 338-48.

Sullivan, Oriel (1997), 'The Division of Housework Among "Remarried" Couples', *Journal of Family Issues*, Vol. 18, No. 2, pp. 205-23.

Sweet, James A. (1973), *Women in the Labor Force*, Seminar Press: New York.

Tarbell, Ida (1913), 'The Cost of Living and Household Management', *Annals of the Academy of Political and Social Science*, Vol.18, p.130.

Taussig, Michael T. (1980), *The Devil and Commodity Fetishism in South America*, University of North Carolina Press: Chapel Hill.

Thompson, E.P. (1963), *The Making of the English Working Class*, Random House: New York.

Thompson, Linda and Walker, Alexis J. (1989), 'Gender in Families: Women and Men in Marriage, Work, and Parenthood', *Journal of Marriage and Family*, Volume 51, November, pp. 845-871.

U.S. Bureau of Labor (1892), *Seventh Annual Report of the Commissioner of Labor*, Vol 2, Part 3. Government Printing Office: Washington, D.C.

U.S. Dept. of Commerce, Bureau of the Census (1951), *Statistical Abstract of the United States*, Government Printing Office: Washington, D.C.

‾‾‾‾‾ (1975), *Historical Statistics of the United States: Colonial Times to 1970*. Government Printing Office: Washington, D.C.

‾‾‾‾‾ (1977), *Statistical Abstract of the United States*, Government Printing Office: Washington, D.C.

‾‾‾‾‾ (1991), *Statistical Abstract of the United States*, Government Printing Office: Washington, D.C.

‾‾‾‾‾ (1993), *Statistical Abstract of the United States*, Government Printing Office: Washington, D.C.

‾‾‾‾‾ (1997), *Statistical Abstract of the United States*, Government Printing Office: Washington, D.C.

U.S. Dept. of Labor, Bureau of Labor Statistics (1978), *Consumer Expenditure Survey Series: Interview Survey, 1972-73: Annual Expenditures and Sources of Income Cross-Classified by Family Characteristics, 1972 and 1973 Combined*, Government Printing Office: Washington, D.C.

‾‾‾‾‾ (1985), *Relative Importance of Components in the Consumer Price Index*, Government Printing Office: Washington, D.C.

‾‾‾‾‾ (1992), *Relative Importance of Components in the Consumer Price Index*, Government Printing Office: Washington, D.C.

U.S. Senate Documents (1910-11, *Report on Condition of Woman and Child Wage-Earners in the U.S. in 19 Volumes,* Government Printing Office: Washington, D.C.

Van Horn, Susan Householder (1988), *Women, Work and Fertility*, New York University Press: New York.

Van Rensselaer, Mrs. John King (1923a), 'Our Social Ladder Its Sound and Rotten Rungs-I', *Ladies' Home Journal*, February.

‾‾‾‾‾ (1923b), 'Our Social Ladder Its Sound and Rotten Rungs-II', *Ladies' Home Journal*, March.

‾‾‾‾‾ (1923b), 'Our Social Ladder Its Sound and Rotten Rungs-III', *Ladies' Home Journal*, April.

Vanek, Joann (1973), 'Keeping Busy: Time Spent on Housework, United States, 1920-1970', doctoral dissertation, University of Michigan: Ann Arbor.

‾‾‾‾‾ (1978), 'Household Technology and Social Status: Rising Living Standards and Status and Residence Differences in Housework', *Technology and Culture*, Vol. 19, No. 3, pp. 361-75.

‾‾‾‾‾ (1980), 'Household, Work, Wage Work, and Sexual Equality', in Berk, Sarah Fenstermaker (ed.), *Women and Household Labor*, Sage: Beverly Hills, pp.275-91

Veblen, Thorstein (1953 [1899]), *The Theory of the Leisure Class,* New American Library: New York.

Vickery, Clair (1979), 'Women's Economic Contribution to the Family', in Smith, Ralph E. (ed.), *The Subtle Revolution: Women at Work*, Urban Institute: Washington, D.C.

Vigil, James Diego (1988), *Barrio gangs: Street Life and Identity in Southern California*, University of Texas Press, Austin.

Viner, Jacob (1991), 'Early Attitudes toward Trade and the Merchant', in Irwin, Douglas A. (ed.), *Essays on the Intellectual History of Economics*, Princeton University Press: Princeton.

Walby, Sylvia (1986), *Patriarchy at Work: Patriarchial and Capitalist Relations in Employment*, University of Minnesota Press: Minneapolis.

Walker, Kathryn (1969), 'Home-Making Still Takes Time', *Journal of Home Economics,* Vol. 61, October.

Walters, Pamela Barnhouse and Rubinson, Richard (1983), 'Educational Expansion and Economic Output in the United States, 1890-1969: A Production Function Analysis', *American Sociological Review*, Vol. 48, August, pp. 480-93.

Wandersee, Winifred D. (1981), *Women's Work and Family Values: 1920-1940*, Harvard University Press: Cambridge.

Weber, Max (1965), *The Sociology of Religion*, Fischoff, Ephraim (translator), Methuen: London.

Wells, David R. (1992), 'Consumerism and the Value of Labor Power', *Review of Radical Political Economics*, Vol. 24, No. 2, pp. 27-34.

West, Candace and Zimmerman, Don H. (1987), 'Doing Gender', *Gender & Society*, Vol. 1, No. 2, pp. 125-151.

White, Lynn K. (1990), 'Determinants of Divorce: A Review of Research in the Eighties', Journal of Marriage and Family, Vol. 52, November, pp. 904-912.

Whittemore, Margaret and Niel, Berniece (1929), *Time Factors in the Business of Homemaking in Rural Rhode Island*, Rhode Island Agriculture Experiment Station Bulletin 221, Rhode Island State College: Kingston, R.I.

Williams, Clair (1929), 'The Position of Women in the Public Schools', *Annals of the American Academy of Political and Social Science*, Vol. 34, pp. 159-65.

Willis, Ellen (1970), 'Consumerism and Women', *Socialist Revolution*, Vol. 1, No. 3.

Wilkie, Jane Riblett (1993), 'Changes in U.S. Men's Attitudes Toward the Family Provider Role, 1972-1989', *Journal of Marriage and Family*, Vol. 7, No. 2, pp. 261-279.

Wilson, Christopher P. (1983), 'The Rhetoric of Consumption: Mass-Market Magazines and the Demise of the Gentle Reader, 1880-1920', in Fox, Richard Wrightman and Lears, T. J. Jackson, *The Culture of Consumption: Critical Essays in American History,* Pantheon: New York, pp.39-64.

Wilson, Maud (1929), *The Time Use of Oregon Farm Home-Makers*, Oregon Agriculture Experiment Station Bulletin 256, Oregon State Agricultural College: Corvallis, OR.

Woodhouse, Chase Going (1929), 'Married Women in Business and the Professions', *Annals of the Academy of Social and Political Science*, Vol. 34, pp. 325-33.

Yergin, Daniel (1991),*The Prize: The Epic Quest for Oil, Money and Power*, Simon and Schuster: New York

Index

class differences 108-09
compensatory 136
conspicuous 61-62, 66, 99
demonstration effect 24, 68
Diderot effect 63-64
luxury goods 66-67
positional goods 68-70
Cowan, Ruth Schwartz 77-78, 80-81
cultural capital 69, 136, 152
culture, youth 67-68
cultures, pre-capitalist European 64

department stores 84-85
divorce 120, 147, 154, 155
domestic servants 102-08
expenditures on 104-07, 109, 113-15
homemaker status 113-15, 121
number of 103-04
race/ethnicity 105-06
support patriarchy 102-03
domestic violence 146, 154
dreams 65
Duesenberry, James 24, 68
Durkheim, Emile 54-56, 59, 65

educational attainment, female 18-19
electricity see living standards
emulation, social 61-63, 136
class differences 136
conformity 62
Engels, Frederick
exploitation of women 34-36, 44
England, Paula 31-32
exchange-value
commodity fetishism 60
consumer sovereignty 60

defined 26n
homemaker's wage 37
expenditure patterns, household 43, 160-63
appliances 108-09, 160-63
domestic service 107-09, 160-63
by presence of housewife 110-15

false consciousness 59
family wage, husband 19, 37, 41-42, 121-31
fertility rates 20-21, 128
Fox, Bonnie 77, 78
Fraad, Harriet 38-40, 44
Frederick, Christine 86, 95, 97
Friedan, Betty 148
Friedman, Milton 51
frozen food 42
functional sociology 33-34

gender identity 120, 143-47
gender ideology 39, 119
gender-creating processes 40-41
Gilman, Charlotte Perkins 28, 82, 89
Goffman, Irving 68
Goldin, Claudia
male wage distribution 131-32
part-time work 93
women's labor force participation 8-13, 15
Gramsci, Antonio 75-76

Hartmann, Heidi 28, 34, 88, 104, 145
Hirsch, Fred 69
Hochschild, Arlie 119-120, 147

household division of labor
anthropological perspectives
32-33
comparative advantage 28-30
functional sociology on 33-34
marital power and 145-46
opportunity cost 30
household-related expenditures
111
housework
isolation 97-98, 136-37, 139-40
menial nature 97-98
professionalization 86
time spent 87-91, 106-07, 110
Huber, Joan 32
Humphries, Jane 7, 41

income
declining working class male
133-37
income distribution by family 100
impact of wives' earnings 134-
35
inequality trends 131-33
income effect 26n, 31, 56
Irish immigrants 58

kitchen 95
Kyrk, Hazel
housework 87, 92, 93
Theory of Consumption 52, 66-
67

labor force participation, women
attitudes
surveyed men 141
surveyed women 141-43
husband's occupation 99-101
marital power and 143-47
measurement
census data 7-8, 13

counting methods 8-10
estimating techniques 11-14
poverty status 121-22

labor supply
econometric analyses 22-24
historical perspectives 57
income effect 26n, 31, 56
substitution effect 26n, 31, 56
supply curve 56-58
labor theory of value 48-49
non-exploitation of homemaker
37
labor-leisure decision 56-58
Ladies' Home Journal
decline of aristocracy 70
effects on housekeeping 94-98
low subscription price 74
Lebergott, Stanley 88, 105
Leibenstein, Harvey 52-53
living standards
appliances 90, 105-110
automobiles 73-74
budget studies 126-31
electricity 90, 73, 122-23
plumbing, indoor 73, 122
luxuries, social *see* consumption
social consensus on 66-67
Lynd, Robert and Helen 73, 74,
99, 123, 126

marital power 143-47
household division of labor
145-46
resource theory 144
Marx, Karl
alienation 59
commodity fetishism 60
exploitation of women 34-36,
44
labor theory of value 48